Louisiana Law

Legends and Laughs

A Collection of Tales
From the Legal Community

Compiled and Edited

by

Frank L. Maraist

and Henry A. Politz

ISBN 0-9719156-0-1

Birdfoot Delta Press
221 Florida Street
Baton Rouge, LA 70801

Printed in the United States of America

DEDICATION

Hank Politz dedicates this book to those who have devoted their lives and their talents to teaching Louisiana law and lawyers, both in the classroom and in the courtroom. Frank Maraist dedicates this book to one of the very best of them, Hank Politz.

TABLE OF CONTENTS

Chapter X

Chapter XI

Chapter XII

Chapter XIII

Chapter XIV

FOREWORD

This collection of stories is the outgrowth of our advancing ages. It occurred that in our 40-plus years in the legal profession, we had seen or heard, and, in some cases, participated in, events whose occurrences should be preserved. Some of the events are instructive, many of them humorous, and a few of them sad. But all of them represent what to us has been a marvelous adventure – participation in the American legal process as students, lawyers, judges and law teachers.

Most of these stories have been contributed by members of the Louisiana bar and bench. They represent events in the study of and in the practice of law that have endured in the memories of busy lawyers and judges. While the great bulk of the stories came from LSU graduates, we made an effort to collect Louisiana law lore from all of the state's legal profession and from the state's other law schools. Almost none of the stories received about the other law schools have been "culled," although we have been forced by good taste and avoidance of repetition to eliminate some of the events that reportedly occurred at the LSU Law School.

We have arranged the stories into loose fitting categories and have provided minimum editing. For the most part, the language actually used by the participants in the events has been retained; to do otherwise would undermine the goal of this book – presenting the Louisiana legal profession as it is. To those who are offended by some of the language, we apologize, and we urge you to avoid lawyers and the practice of law.

Gathering the stories in this book has been a bittersweet experience. The disappointment has been learning how many of our contemporaries in the law are gone and how many more are no longer actively in the practice of law. The joy has been in finding so many more of those contemporaries who are still making great contributions to the profession we love so well. It reminds us of the words of a poem, which meant nothing in our youth but so much more now.

i

We are not now that strength which in old days
moved Heaven and earth

That which we are, we are

One equal temper of heroic hearts, made weak by
time and fate, but strong in will

To strive, to seek, to find and not to yield.*

This book also is dedicated to those heroic hearts in appreciation for the joy the authors have felt in learning that they have not yet yielded.

The authors express special thanks to their patient and long-suffering "right hands," Ruth Elkins and Linda Duplessis, for their assistance in preparing this work.

We hope you enjoy reading these stories half as much as we've enjoyed collecting and presenting them.

Frank L. Maraist

Henry A. Politz

Baton Rouge, Louisiana

February 1, 2002

* Alfred Lord Tennyson: Ulysses

CHAPTER I
THE LAW PROFESSORS

To the average law student, the law professor is a larger than life living legend. One reason is that most of the memorable law professors were or are brilliant, articulate, sometimes witty and usually intimidating. Probably every living lawyer can remember the first days in law school, the first time he or she was called upon to recite, and the agony of the first final exam. Another reason why so many law professors are legendary is that the give and take of learning and applying the law in a classroom setting brings out the best and worst in men and women – student and teacher alike.

Every law school has its "legends." If you went to Ole Miss, within a few days of your arrival you knew or heard of John Fox. If you went to the University of Texas, you marveled in the presence or in the memory of Page Keeton, Charley McCormick and Leon Green. As a young law teacher 30+ years ago, one of your authors was privileged to occupy an office next to that of Dean Green. At that time, he was in his eighties but continued to teach torts at UT by special act of the Texas legislature. The author felt particularly close to Dean Green because the author planned to become a torts teacher and also because they were both native Louisianians. Dean Green's student accomplishments rivaled his career as a law teacher. The story goes that during his freshman year at UT, Dean Green sat in on upper class courses and at the end of his first year, he took and passed the Texas bar. During his second year he worked part-time in the city attorney's office and in his senior year in law school, he served as the city attorney of Austin. Dean Green is best remembered in Louisiana as the architect of the "duty/risk" approach which continues to dominate Louisiana tort law.

Our collection of stories about law professors begins with Dean Paul Macarius "Mac" Hebert. Mac served as dean of the Loyola law school in 1930-31, and as dean of the LSU law school for 35 years thereafter. He was the architect of the LSU Law Center which now bears his name, and died at a speaker's podium seeking additional funds to promote the Center. Those of us who knew him as his students and as faculty colleagues remember his penetrating mind, his perfect diction, and his ability to deliver a grammatically perfect

1

extemporaneous speech. However, there was a side to him few of us knew. It is revealed in the following story from his son-in-law, Baton Rouge attorney Charles McCowan.

> I married Mary Hebert, Dean Hebert's daughter. I loved Dr. Hebert, but suspected he was absent minded; when he was Dean at Loyola, he once walked the garbage can from his house to school rather than just to the curb, and he frequently forgot that he had driven to school and would catch a ride home. I suspect that I did not make much of an impression on him as a son in law. We had been married several years and had a child when Mary graduated from the College of Arts and Sciences at LSU. Graduation was held in the "cowbarn." As the candidates were lining up for their march to receive their degrees, Dr. Hebert, full robes flowing, ran up to Mary and, holding an open graduation program, asked, "Mary, why aren't you graduating?" When she asked what he was talking about, he said, "There is no Mary Hebert in the program." She reminded him that she had been married for several years, and that he should look up her name that way.

During his lengthy tenure, Dean Hebert often came to the assistance of his students. Some of that assistance is chronicled elsewhere in this work.

Wex Malone, a nationally renowned torts scholar, spent 35 years delighting the students at LSU. Here are some of the memories.

> In the 1950s, smoking was permitted in the LSU law classrooms, and Professor Malone was a chain smoker. Prior to lighting up, Wex would take a cigarette from the pack and twirl it in his hands, from the left hand to the right hand and back again. Often he would lose track of where the filter was. Several times during the course of the year he would put the cigarette into his mouth backwards, and, consumed with interest in his subject matter, he would light the filter. We were all so

intimidated by him that no one would tell him what was about to happen. He would leave the class muttering about the stupidity of his students in not advising him that he was about to light the filter end of his cigarette.

On the morning that we took our final examination in Torts I, he came to class and purposefully started to light the filter end of his cigarette. A unanimous cry came from the class warning him of the impending tragedy. He left the classroom realizing that we had learned something during the semester.

Leslie Schiff
Opelousas

One struggling student was having difficulty grasping tort concepts in Malone's class and he began going to Malone's home for a bit of after hours tutoring in preparation for the forthcoming examination. The student had the benefit of a number of such sessions before taking the exam, and felt he had greatly benefitted from them. After the exam, when the grades were posted (there was no effort to conceal who received what grade back in those days), this student was dismayed to see that he had made an "F" in Malone's course. He went to see the professor to discuss with him the reason for his failure. Upon his return, we asked him what happened in the interview. He stated that he had asked Professor Malone why he had made an "F" in the course, and Malone's response was "because that's the lowest grade I could give you."

Judge Jim Trimble
Lake Charles

When I was in Wex Malone's Torts class in the fall semester, 1972 (by the way, I'm certain that Wex is spinning in his grave knowing that I now teach Torts), we were discussing consent, one of Wex's favorite topics. At this particular point in time, Professor Malone had recently undergone cataract surgery, and a dark lens on his glass frame shielded the affected eye. After raising one of his typically difficult hypotheticals on informed consent, Wex called on one of our "one semester" law school classmates who loved to expound on the mysteries of the law while solving them. As Wex craned his neck to focus his good eye on his prey, he heard, "Mr. Malone, I was a pre-med major prior to coming to law school, and I've worked in hospitals between semesters." Wex leaned forward to listen more intently, but said nothing. The silence in the room was like being inside the eye of a hurricane. "I've been in the operating room, and I've assisted with numerous procedures," blurted our soon to be "road scholar." "Because of my extensive medical background, I would hate to take advantage of you by answering your question," he continued. By this time, Malone was almost out of his chair as his head swivelled to finally focus his lone working eye on our classmate. I can still hear Wex's raspy retort, "Try me!"

Professor Tom Richard
Southern University Law Center

In my freshman Torts class, taught by Professor Malone, there were two brothers (or cousins – at any rate, they had the same last name, that being Jewel) named Kenneth and John. With what surely was a random selection, the good professor called upon Kenneth to recite. No response was forthcoming. A quick reference to the seating chart, then to the empty chair, revealed that Kenneth was absent. Undaunted, and already looking at the midpoint of his roll book, Professor Malone tried again. "John Jewel," he cried. No response. Another glance to the seating chart and then to the appropriate chair revealed that John also was absent.. In his quintessential deadpan, Professor Malone intoned dryly, "We seem to have lost both our Jewels today." The class erupted in laughter.

Stan Bardwell
Baton Rouge

Mrs. Harriet "Ma" Daggett was one of America's first female law teachers and one of LSU's enduring legends. This story illustrates a typical day in one of Ma's classes.

We were studying family law with the legendary Mrs. Daggett at the LSU Law School right after World War II. Our discussion reached Civil Code Article

137, which provided that the wife could not remarry until ten months after the dissolution of her preceding marriage. Classmate Walter Peters, who later became a judge, asked Mrs. Daggett why the limitation was set at ten months. Mrs. Daggett showed mock anger as she advised him: "Mr. Peters, it's difficult enough teaching you family law without also teaching you the facts of life."

Harvey Posner
Baton Rouge

(The authors did not recall Article 137, although it was not repealed until 1970. Those of us who began practicing in the 1950s are confident that the article was honored more in its breach).

J. Denson Smith, a/k/a "Big Red," taught Contracts, Obligations, Sales and Insurance at LSU during four decades. His mastery of the Socratic method reduced to tears most of the mere mortals among the LSU student body. "Big Red" (the origin of the name is obscure, but the most persistent story is that one morning, after a night of carousing, he was visited at his office by his female companion of the evening before, who asked his secretary if "Big Red" was in) also had a caustic wit and a penchant for golf. The following stories capture in part the magnificence of this legend.

There was a certain member of our class of 1961 who didn't make it all the way through both semesters. The first final we took was Dr. Bennett's criminal law exam. Approximately 2-1/2 hours into that four hour exam this worthy simply got up and walked out after turning in his Blue Book and proclaiming that he was finished. Needless to say, that sent a shiver down everyone else's back. Throughout the rest of the exams, the same thing more or less occurred and after each exam when he returned to the law dorm and a discussion was held about the questions on the exam and what was the correct answer, our confident classmate generally disagreed with everyone, which led us all to believe that either he was the next Oliver Wendell Holmes and we were in deep trouble or he had insights beyond mortal ken. When the grades from the first semester were posted (you'd get sued for that today), he was at the bottom end of the class. Our friend was incensed by this and made appointments with each of the professors, demanding an explanation as to why he had done so poorly in their classes. When he got to "Big Red," I overheard what followed (at that time, I was working as Professor Malone's research assistant and happened to be in the carrels right outside of Smith's office). After listening to the demand for an explanation as to why our friend had "foxed" obligations, "Big Red" inquired as to what grade the student had made with Professor Malone and was told that it was a "fox" as well. And Dean McMahon? Dog. And so on, until the pack of dogs and foxes were complete except for legal bibliography where, in response to Professor Smith's inquiry, our worthy proudly announced that he made a "C". At that point "Big Red" leaned back in his chair and said, "Ahhhhh. I perceive the mistake you made. You simply focused too much time and attention on legal bibliography at the expense of your other classes."

Tim McNamara
Lafayette

Professor Smith once called upon a student to recite on a particular case in contracts. The student responded by stating that "In this case the plaintiff sued the defendant." With that he stopped, and J. Denson sat patiently waiting for him to continue. After what seemed an interminable period of time, Professor Smith slowly removed his glasses, fixed the student with a most formidable glare, and asked,

"Mr. _____, were there other unusual aspects about this particular case?"

Judge Jim Trimble
Lake Charles

Peyton Parker of Baton Rouge provides these two stories which capture the charisma of "Big Red":

> In the summer of 1950, fellow student Tres Owen and I underwent military training together at Fort Benning. At the end of the summer, we were allowed to return to the Law School to complete our studies. In my conversations with Tres that summer, we talked a great deal about law school and particularly about being "under the gun" by Professor Denson Smith. I told Tres that I did not have to worry about that because I was listed on the roll sheets as "J.P. Parker" and right beneath was J.V. Parker (John). I told Tres that if I was not prepared, I would simply wait it out and John Parker would always answer. Tres and I both obtained a deferment to finish another semester of law school before we were required to go on active duty. That semester found me in sales under Professor Smith. About the third class, Dr. Smith took off his glasses in his inimitable style, looked at me, asked a question, and said "J. Peyton Parker, Jr." Then he smiled, and I knew what Tres had done.

One story, perhaps apocryphal, was that "Big Red" played golf frequently with one of his students who was an excellent golfer and who once beat "Big Red" in an important match. Filled with pride, the student golfer extended his hand and suggested to "Big Red" that there should be no hard feelings over the outcome. At the end of the semester, the two were playing golf together again and the student asked "Big Red" if he had finished grading the finals. "Big Red," addressing the ball at the tee, replied in the affirmative. The student asked what grade he had made. "Big Red" said in his dry, crisp voice. "You made an F." He then drove his ball into the fairway, looked up, and said "No hard feelings."

Judge Jacques Weiner of New Orleans provides this vignette:

> The late professor Mitchell Franklin taught at the Tulane Law School over the course of five decades, and was legendary for, among other things, his own irreverent and intimidating version of the Socratic method. He was revered by 3Ls, chuckled about by 2Ls, and abjectly feared by 1Ls. An incident in Professor Franklin's 1958 1L Contracts class provided a humorous exception to the "realm of fear and trembling" otherwise pervading the professor's classroom. Consistent with Professor Franklin's practice of impressing on 1Ls how parochial, poorly educated, and unsophisticated a lot they all were, his opening class was devoted to, among other things, pointing out how miserably equipped these "greenhorns" were from the standpoint of foreign language skills. Professor Franklin began by asking for a show of hands from those who were fluent in each of a number of modern Western languages, such as French, Spanish, Italian and German, pausing after each to comment negatively on how few hands were raised. He then queried as to the ancient Greek and Latin, with more dismal results. Finally, Professor Franklin asked that each student who was fluent in any language that he had not named raise his or her hand. Only a smattering went up and, resorting to the seating chart, he called on each to identify the language. When he got to the last row, he looked at the chart, identified the hand-raiser, and asked, "Yes, Mr. Preedy, in what other language are you fluent?" To which Mr. Preedy replied, "Thai." At that, Professor Franklin went into a diatribe about how marvelous it was that Mr. Preedy was fluent in Thai while the balance of the parochial and provincial Louisiana students (who

predominated the class) could speak only English – and that not too well. However, what everyone but the professor knew was that Mr. Preedy was Siamese, had been born and raised in Bangkok, and Thai was his native tongue!

Another vignette of a Tulane law professor, dating back to the late 20s or 30s, comes from Jim Van Hook of Shreveport.

> The teaching techniques of one of the law school professors, Dr. Beutel, was to state the facts in a real or imaginary case and elicit the opinions of those in his class as to what a court should decide. A story about one such class – which took place before I attended law school – was being repeated after my entry and involved Sam Herold, who was from Shreveport and later was a well-known and respected Shreveport lawyer. This particular class met from 11:00 a.m. to noon, just before the recess for lunch, and some classes began again at 1:00 p.m. The first bell for lunch recess rang and Dr. Beutel kept asking for opinions. The second and final bell for lunch rang, and Dr. Beutel continued to seek opinions. He wanted somebody to say that in the instant case, the statute of limitations had run, but no one obliged. Sam Herold thought Dr. Beutel had not heard the bells, Sam was hungry and he wanted his lunch, so he sought and got Dr. Beutel's attention and said, "Dr. Beutel, times up." Dr. Beutel replied: "Yes, by God, I've been trying for 30 minutes to get someone to say the statute of limitations had run."

Those who have taught on a regular basis over a long period of time are familiar with the phenomenon: after a while every student reminds you of a former student. The "former student syndrome" becomes more acute when the names of the students are similar. This syndrome hit Dr. Dale Bennett, a great teacher and human being, in his third decade of teaching at LSU.

On the first day of a corporations class, he observed a student (Files) who (to Dr. Bennett, at least) looked remarkably like a student of an earlier generation (Pipes). On the first day, before the roll was compiled, Dr. Bennett looked at Files, recognized him as Pipes, and called upon him to recite. Files, unwilling to excite the professor's wrath (at least at that stage of the game), responded as Pipes. When the same thing occurred several days later, Files reminded Dr. Bennett that he was not Pipes. By this time however, Files' classmates had gotten into the act. The roll sheet was being compiled from signatures on a tablet passed around at the first few meetings, and each day a student would write in Pipes' name. When the official roll sheet came out, it contained both names – Files and Pipes. Dr. Bennett, convinced that Pipes was there, called upon him, looking directly at Files. Files recited. However, the matter was not at an end. The students continued to check the box indicating Pipes' presence at every class, and when Pipes' name came up in the rotation for recitation, Dr. Bennett called upon Files, looking at him and expecting a response. Finally, near the end of the semester, Files, who because of Dr. Bennett's Files-Pipes confusion had recited twice as many times as his fellow students, could take it no more. Called upon as Pipes, he blurted out: "Dr. Bennett, I've told you again and again, I'm not Pipes, my name is Files." "Of course," Dr. Bennett replied, "you're Files." Then looking around the classroom, he asked "Pipes, Pipes, where are you?" That was one of the few classes in which students walked out laughing before the bell rang.

The Files-Pipes episode prompted one Law School poet to pen this verse:

> There is a professor named Bennett,
>
> Whose class roll showed more than the limit.
>
> Where he sat we don't know,
>
> For Pipes came incognito,
>
> But to Bennett, when class met, Pipes was in it.

Mel Dakin taught at the LSU Law School for 30 years and during that time came to be regarded as the ultimate gentleman who would go to great lengths to avoid embarrassing a student. The traditional story is that he once asked a student whether the plaintiff had won or lost the case the professor had assigned for classroom discussion. When the student replied "he lost," Professor Dakin responded: "Very good. Of course, you would have been more correct if you had said he won."

Alan Fishbein of Baton Rouge reports a similar Dakin response. In a tax course, the professor asked a student whether a particular issue would be a deduction or an exemption on a tax return. The student responded "it would be an exemption." Professor Dakin, after chortling, looked at the student and said "almost right".

George Pugh, one of LSU's most brilliant graduates, joined the faculty as a young man in 1950 and served until his retirement in 1994. During that time, his facility as a penetrating legal analyst (which he applied to both students and his fellow teachers) and his genuine love for people endeared him to several generations of Louisiana lawyers. Unfortunately, Professor Pugh suffers from a congenital eye disease which has severely restricted his vision during most of his adult life. (His brother, Tom, suffered from the same malady but also made great contributions to Louisiana law and lore; some of Tom's escapades are chronicled in Chapter VI).

Here are some recollections about Professor Pugh.

While attending LSU Law School, I was in Professor Pugh's Evidence class when he called upon a motorcycle helmet to recite. I was one row behind and two or three seats over when a student motorcyclist came in on a rainy day, put his poncho over the back of the adjoining, vacant chair to drip dry, and placed his helmet on the desk/table. When class began, Professor Pugh immediately called upon the student wearing the poncho and motorcycle helmet, and couldn't understand why he wasn't getting a response. After asking his question, prodding, then taunting, and finally challenging the absent and very silent Mr. Blank, the suppressed chuckles in the classroom clued him in that something was amiss. Finally he asked: "O.K., What's so funny?" When told, he agreed that it was pretty funny, and observed that he wondered why the "student never moved."

Michael Bordelon
Mandeville

At the 1976 Louisiana State Bar Association meeting, one of my fellow graduates from the class of 1975 arrived at the LSU Law Alumni party in a "liquid state." Upon seeing Professor Pugh, our new lawyer made a somewhat circuitous route to George to thank him for his law school education and to praise his considerable teaching talents. After several eternities passed, Professor Pugh, unable to take any more praise, said, "Mr. _____, for the first time I do believe that I can see you better than you can see me!"

Professor Tom Richard
Southern University Law Center

Professor Pugh was a master at quizzing students in the classroom, but his technique didn't end there. He delighted in quizzing younger faculty about the law when they met in the faculty lounge, and, in many cases, "tearing up" the young faculty member's analysis with his keen insight. One day, he met a young, untenured faculty member in the faculty lounge and asked him, "---------------, what did you think of the ----------- case (an important recent decision in a field of law which they both taught)?" The young faculty member, seeking to avoid confrontation and probably defeat, responded that he had not yet read the case. George was undaunted; his next comment was, "Well, if you had read it, what would you think about it?"

Professor Pugh's physical handicap and mental prowess are reflected in this 1950s ditty about him penned by one of his students and preserved by another, Bernard Kramer of Alexandria:

> "There is a young man named Pugh,
> Who captains the staff of the Law Review.
> Though reliant on glasses,
> He still makes jackasses,
> Of all would-be lawyers like you.

Professor Saul Litvinoff, the "guru" of the Louisiana version of the civil law, has taught at LSU since 1965. During that time, both his wit and his wisdom have left his students in awe. Here is a recollection of each:

> A law student who sustained a broken ankle continued to attend classes. However, to accommodate his infirmity, he sat on the back row, away from the other students. During one of Professor Litvinoff's classes, the student (whom we'll call Watson) sought to ease the strain on his foot by placing his leg on the table next to him. Professor Litvinoff, observing this, called out, "Mr. Watson, I see you have your leg up. What is your question?"

> Allen Bergeron
> Baton Rouge

> Within the first week of law school, Professor Litvinoff, using the Socratic method, asked a question to which Tim Cerniglia responded. Professor Litvinoff then observed that the answer sounded like a response that a divinity student would give, and from that day forward he referred to Cerniglia as Father Cerniglia. On the last day of class, a number of students, including Joe Ferguson, Jacqueline Cooper, Cerniglia and I, borrowed a habit from the Catholic Life Center on campus. Cerniglia dressed in the habit in the men's room at the law school. As class began, Professor Litvinoff looked

around the room and commented that it was a shame that Father Cerniglia was not here for the last day of class. A few minutes later, Cerniglia entered the classroom in full garb. Professor Litvinoff, perhaps for the first time, was speechless for a few seconds. Then he looked at Cerniglia and said, "I'm glad that you are here; however, had you not been here, I was going to take the students to see the visually obscured movie at the Varsity. However, since a man of your standing is present, I can no longer do that." He then finished the semester without any further ado.

Alan Fishbein
Baton Rouge

My section of the first year class had Professor Litvinoff for Obligations. He was a wonderful and incredible teacher in that he had the text (which he wrote) memorized and he would lecture without any materials before him. One day, as he was teaching us in a room without windows, the electricity went off. Because the door to our classroom was open, we could see that all other classes had been dismissed. However, Professor Litvinoff did not stutter. He continued to lecture, and we continued to sit there. He did not need the lights. We, of course, did need lights to take notes, but no one was about to stop Professor Litvinoff. After class, we lamented how "lucky" we had been to have, at the time the electricity went out, a teacher who had memorized his course.

Kirsten David
Baton Rouge

Dean Sutherland of New Orleans, who now teaches part-time at the LSU Law Center, offers this recollection of Howard L'Enfant, who has taught at LSU for over 30 years and who has served as associate dean and as interim dean.

In 1974, L'Enfant was teaching Federal Courts at the LSU Law Center. The casebook contained two sequential, but apparently inconsistent, decisions regarding a fine point of federal removal practice. One case was entitled "Climax Chemical Co. v. C.F. Braun & Co." while the other case name has been lost in the fog of time.

Professor L'Enfant discussed the two cases, but I remained confused about the distinction between their holdings. I requested additional clarification from Professor L'Enfant. The following is a verbatim quote of his response:

"Well, you have to understand that <u>Climax</u> is an unusual case."

When the peals of laughter from the less-sensitive members of the class finally subsided, Professor L'Enfant observed:

"I really blew that one."

Once again, the class erupted. The crimson flush on Professor L'Enfant's face and neck deepened. In huge letters, he wrote on the chalk board: 'GO HOME!!!"

After the rest of the class left, I approached Professor L'Enfant to seek an individual response to my query. He refused to speak, shaking his head "no" and pointing to the words on the chalk board.

To this day, I don't know which case was correct.

Mike Rubin, of Baton Rouge, presently serving as the president of the State Bar, contributes this story:

Bill Crawford is now a senior professor at LSU, where he has served for 36 years. Many years ago, when Crawford was a young professor, he played in a student/faculty softball game and, in a fit of exuberance, rounded third base at a high speed. With the ball whizzing to the catcher, Crawford attempted to elude being tagged out by sliding into home plate. Unfortunately, Bill broke his leg in the process and spent the next few weeks encased in a large cast that extended from his thigh to his toes. On his first day back at class, Bill hobbled in on crutches, propped his leg up on a chair and proceeded to start the lecture. Before he could begin, however, a male voice from the rear of the classroom yelled, "Professor, how's your sex life?"

Without missing a beat, Bill responded, "The only extremity I broke was my leg." He then continued as the class laughed nigh hysterically.

Professor Athanasios Yiannapolous, better known as "Yippie," taught at LSU from 1958 to 1979 and, after retiring, became a member of the Tulane faculty, where he still holds forth. Ben Hanchey of Monroe reports that on one occasion Yippie was teaching property at LSU during the period that the movie *Zorba the Greek* was playing. One of the students asked Professor Yiannopoulos if he had seen *Zorba the Greek*, to which Yippie replied, "I *am* Zorba the Greek."

One of the authors of this work who has taught law for over 30 years has carefully "culled" stories submitted about some of his classroom antics. However, the fleeting spirit of humility compels that we report this one. Years ago I was teaching at the Ole Miss Law School (an experience in itself for a long-time Tiger). The classroom in the old law building (they've since built a modern structure) was a converted library, with vertical support beams near the center of the room. I had been provided with a seating chart, a paper with a series of squares representing the placement of seats in the classroom and containing the names of the students assigned to those seats. As I roamed the classroom expounding on some timely topic (I think it was Evidence), I paused to elicit an answer from a student sitting nearby. Glancing quickly at the chart to learn his name, I called out, looking directly at the student: "How about that, Mr. Post?" When my question drew no reaction or response, I moved closer and asked more emphatically: "Well, Mr. Post, what about it. Don't you have anything to say?" Again, no response. My next comment: "Mr. Post, this is a law school class. Don't you want to participate?" The student's response, almost flippant, was "I'm not Mr. Post." I then looked at the seating chart to learn, to my chagrin, that the word Post had been written into the seating chart to indicate the point (next to the student's seat) at which a post (the vertical support beam) blended in with the subsequently installed classroom seats. I confessed error to the students, who, needless to say, called the unfortunate student "Mr. Post" for the remainder of his law school career.

CHAPTER II

THE LAW STUDENT

1. Promises

The law is not for everybody, as many a law student learns during his or her first semester. But that's not always bad. One LSU student was at the very bottom of his class in his senior year. He wrote a poor paper for Ma Daggett on his final exam, and she was about to give him an F. He was a very likable fellow and he went to Ma and begged her to give him a passing grade. She finally relented and told him that she would do so, but only if he would swear to her that he would never practice law a day of his life. He kept that promise, went on to follow a business career, and became the wealthiest member of his law class.

Former Governor Dave Treen, now practicing in New Orleans, tells the reverse story.

Before I went to Law School, I was in the College of Arts and Sciences at Tulane, planning to attend law school on the program that permitted one to enter law school after three years, and the first year of law school would complete the requirements for a BA degree. I was required to take a science course and I chose physics.

That could have been one of the worst mistakes in my life because I found physics extremely difficult. I was not doing well in the course. Towards the end of the semester, the physics professor called me into his office to inform me that I was failing. He said that he had heard that I was planning to go to law school, and I confirmed that it was my intention to go to Tulane Law School. He then said, as accurately as I can recall his words: "If you promise me you will go to law school, and not pursue engineering or some other scientific profession, I will give you a passing grade." Of course, I made the solemn promise, and he gave me a grade of "D"!

As it turns out, in the legal profession, a good knowledge of physics and other scientific fields can be of great benefit. In any event, I still thank the physics professor for his magnanimity.

2. Confidence and Overconfidence

Perhaps every entering law school class has a student who brims over with confidence. Students at LSU in the mid-1950s remember the late B. Roy Liuzza, a/k/a "Big Julie," who announced confidently after his first final examinations that he had made all As! One must remember that at that time, the forced attrition (flunk out) rate was about 60%, underscoring the absurdity of his claim. And, of course, he was wrong: he made four As and a B!

Former Governor Dave Treen tells of a similar student at Tulane:

> At the end of our first year of law school in 1948, I mentioned to a friend, who shall remain anonymous, that I thought the examinations were very difficult, and I was greatly troubled that I may have flunked out of law school. My friend responded in words about like this: "Are you kidding? They were a cinch. I couldn't believe how easy they were!"
>
> A few weeks later, we received our grades. I had passed all of my courses, and my friend had flunked out of law school!
>
> I believe he went on to a very successful business career, which means he may have been the real winner.

3. Learning the Language

Law students spend most of their first year learning "terms of art," i.e., words which mean one thing in the "outside world" and another to lawyers and judges. Often the students have difficulty mastering the terms. Camille Cutrone of New Orleans recalls that one day after a class in either Obligations or Civil Procedure at Tulane in which the hypothecary action was mentioned, he overheard one student, who apparently thought the professor had said "apothecary action," ask another student why the Code had a section dealing with drugstore operators.

At LSU one student, obviously ignorant of French, sat through the entire course in Obligations and wrote on his final exam about the "stipulation 403" which, for the uninitiated, we translate to "stipulation pour autri."

Caldwell Roberts of Shreveport shares this "blooper":

> Don Beckner, Frank Foil and I were sitting on the back row of a class in constitutional law. The subject was the Mann Act. The Professor asked Beckner where Congress obtained the power and authority to enact such legislation, and Beckner replied, "Professor, interstate commerce is defined as intercourse among the States."

4. Schmoozing

It once was called "brown nosing" (the origin of that term should be obvious to any reader) and in later years it is referred to as "schmoozing" – the art of "sucking up" to the professor to assure an improved grade. There are two kinds of law students - -those who "schmooze" and those who hate those who "schmooze." Hank Bruser of Alexandria relates this tale:

> Every class has a "brown noser" who loves to hear himself talk, and who sits on the front row asking inane questions at every opportunity. Our freshman class was no exception. Out of weeks of classmates' ignored hints and even joking requests that our irritating peer "button his lip" was born a counterattack which included scratching his given name off of the roll sheet that was circulated in each class, and substituting nicknames such as "Kiss Ass," "Motor Mouth" and finally "Chief Judge," which eventually stuck. "Instructions" were hand printed on the top of the roll sheet directing each student to

indicate in the blank beside his or her name whether he or she wanted the "Chief Judge" to stop asking questions and making comments in class. "Polls" were taken in the margins of the roll sheets to determine those in favor of and against further questions or intelligent observations by the Chief Judge. Nothing slowed him down. One day his name and all areas surrounding his name on the roll sheets were completely blacked out so that he had no space to place his initials reflecting his presence. He doggedly carried on. The next day a student brought a razor blade to class and physically cut the "Chief Judge's" name off all of the roll sheets. That afternoon as the students were rising to leave Yippie's introduction to Civil Law class, the distraught Chief Judge raised his hand and asked Yippie if he were still registered in the class. Suddenly, you could have heard a pin drop. Yippie inquired, "Why do you ask?" "Because my name has been cut off the roll sheet all day," said the Chief Judge, to which Yippie responded, "Obviously you ask too many questions!" Classmates rolled in the aisles.

Even the professor came to despise one schmoozer. At the LSU Law School in the mid-fifties, Dr. Eric Voegelin, a famed international scholar, taught a mandatory course called "Institutions." Dr. Voegelin spoke at a level of abstraction and with an accent which made it impossible for nearly any of the students to understand what he was talking about. The class was beginning to panic near the end of the semester: the only thing they apparently knew about the course was that Justinian borrowed heavily from Plato, and they were trying to devise some strategy to convert that into a D on the final exam.

Even more panicky was the class "brown noser," whose usual practice was to "schmooze" the professor openly in class while in the process of asking a question. The class reached its final week, and the "brown noser" did not understand enough to ask a question. Unwilling to give up what he thought was an essential advantage, he finally raised his hand. Dr. Voegelin immediately lit up, as this was the first student question of the semester. Our schmoozer fired his volley: "Dr. Voegelin, you are a fantastic teacher and we are all so lucky to have you teach us. I've enjoyed this class more than any other. I only have one question." "Ja, ja, vut is it," Dr. Voegelin inquired eagerly. The schmoozer: "Who came first – Plato or Justinian?" Dr. Voegelin's red face turned beet red, and he bellowed "dummkopf, I'm not going to tell you."

5.   Recitations

Classroom recitation is the bete noire of law school students. If the student is unprepared and is caught, he is punished, and if he is prepared, he gets pummeled by a professor with superior knowledge and the Socratic "stick." The latter attack sometimes brings a law career to a premature end. Consider this story.

Professor William Crawford at the LSU Law School was going into great detail about an unfortunate accident in which a passenger awaiting the arrival of a train (was this <u>Palsgraf</u>?) slipped on a banana peel. The student who was being questioned at the time inquired of Professor Crawford as to the possibility that the peel had been placed on the floor by a passerby a short time before the fall. Professor Crawford, ever patient, again described how the banana peel was brownish-blackish, grimy, sandy, etc., when the student interrupted him and asked, "Well, couldn't someone have just eaten that banana and placed that peel on the floor?" Professor Crawford looked rather exasperated and replied, "Ms. Jones, you must run with a different crowd than I do."

Two weeks later I bumped into Ms. Jones in the hall between classes and asked how she was doing. She responded, "Great, I just resigned from law school!"

Tommy Zentner
Monroe

At LSU Law School in the fifties a student generally was allowed a number of UPs (unprepareds slips) which allowed him to attend class although unprepared. One trick was to place a UP on the far end of the professor's desk (or on the floor next to it) and if called upon, claim and find the UP, but if not called upon, retrieve the UP after class and save it for another day. Getting caught in class unprepared and without having turned in a UP was a serious offense which could cost up to 15% of the final grade. That explains why things like the following event occurred on occasion.

In olden times (1956) Dr. Dale Bennett's class was in the "Junior" classroom, the only room where smoking was allowed in the old Law School building. He called on Frank Maraist to report on one of the assigned cases. Frank, always courageous and a gambler, had not put a UP slip on Dr. Bennett's desk before class.

How did Frank solve his problem, considering that he had not read the assignment and couldn't fake his response? He simply reached to his left and grabbed the brief prepared by the author of this note. As Maraist began to read the brief, I took out my cigarette lighter and set fire to the brief. Of course, this brought on quite a scene on the last row of the classroom. Frank tried to put the fire out, at the same time cursing under his breath his unwilling benefactor and continuing to read the stolen brief.

The interesting part was that Dr. Bennett knew something unusual was happening but Frank was able to avoid detection by quenching the fire and reading through the smoke of the burning paper and the cigarettes on the back row. And also because I didn't rat on him, but exercised street justice.

Judge James E. Clark
Shreveport

Bob Donovan of Shreveport submits this memory of the UP system:

J. Denson Smith, affectionately known as "Big Red," was strict on the use of the UP slips. Some few students

would play the odds and attend class unprepared, hoping
not to be called on. Few dared to do so in Big Red's class.
Art Haack was the exception. He would attend class
unprepared, expecting not to be called on. Big Red was
careful with UPs, recording each in his daily log, and
saving the papers until after the class. One day Art, who
had one remaining unused UP, brazenly chose not to use
it. Bad things happened. On the toughest case of the day,
where "winging it" was simply impossible, Art was called
on. Art, who had a speech impediment, slowly stuttered
that he had turned in a UP slip. Big Red looked at his daily
log, but there was no mark by Art's name for that date. He
then examined the stack of UP slips given that morning.
He said: " Mr. Haack, I do not have a UP slip from you for
this class." Art looked astounded and said, "Mr. Smith, I
have been made the brunt of a cruel joke." Mr. Smith
responded very slowly: "Very well, but I suggest that you
take great care to make certain that you are not made the
brunt of such a cruelty in this class again."

There was no playing fast and loose with UP slips
in that class for the remainder of that semester. Art, the
story goes, did not even use the third one he had
remaining.

As one might expect, a great classroom recitation story
involved Harmon Drew, an incomparable musician, entrepreneur
and comedian, and now a state appellate judge. Mike Pulaski of
New Orleans tells this story.

In the old law building there were long tables with
individual wooden chairs for the students. These chairs
were not bolted down and could be moved around (or
kicked back). During Professor Mel Dakin's constitutional
law class, Harmon (who sat on the last row with me and
Al Provosty – nothing suspicious there) was asked to
explain the commerce clause by using a "house that Jack
built" analogy. Harmon, who was the lead singer and
organ player of the rock band, Ivy Peoples Medicine Show,

during our undergraduate and law school years (and subsequent years as well), wasn't quite giving Mr. Dakin the answer he needed, so Mr. Dakin point blank asked Harmon if he knew the "house that Jack built." Harmon's eyes lit up and he told Mr. Dakin he knew all about the "house that Jack built." With that, he immediately jumped up, kicked his chair back and started mimicking playing a piano on top of the table and singing Aretha Franklin's popular hit "This is the House that Jack Built." After singing the entire first verse, Harmon sat down, feeling quite proud of himself. All of us were about to "bust a gut" trying to hold in the laughter. Mr. Dakin, being the calm gentleman he was, told Harmon that while that was very nice recitation on the "house that Jack built," it "wasn't quite what he had in mind." At that point the entire class broke out in uncontrolled laughter.

A less humorous response met the following student recitation:

Carlos Lazarus taught Successions and Donations and Common Law Property during my student days. One day in a Successions class, the answer given by the student reciting was not satisfactory. This elicited a mild, but clear, rebuff from Mr. Lazarus, with the observation that the student (whose identity is to me lost in the mist of history) should spend more time preparing for class, including a better review of the applicable civil code articles. The student, his frustration overcoming his discretion, blurted out that if the "xx%&" index to the Code (that being understood by all in his hearing to mean the Dainow Code, which had just been published and was used as the text for the class) had been arranged in a logical, coherent, and otherwise reasonable and responsible manner, he could have found just which articles might have been applicable to the question he had just failed to answer satisfactorily. In his thick broken English, Professor Lazarus noted that he had compiled and organized the index to the Dainow Code and would be happy to receive suggestions for its improvement. You could have heard a pin drop at that revelation, which none of us knew before that moment. The student in question sank from view under his desk.

Stan Bardwell
Baton Rouge

Jim Van Hook of Shreveport reports this tale of a tardy but quick-thinking Tulane student of yore:

There were a good many Jewish boys in the student body of Tulane Law School when I was there, and, of course, they assiduously celebrated all of the numerous Jewish holidays. On one such holiday a student with a very Anglo Saxon name was marked absent at a class that began about 10:00 in the morning. When the class was almost exactly half over, the door opened and in came the missing student. The professor stopped casting his pearls of wisdom and said, "Welcome, Mr. Smith. We thought you were observing a holiday." Student Smith promptly and without hesitation replied, "Yes, professor, but only my mother is Jewish and I therefore take note of only half the holiday."

A professor was explaining to a junior law school class some of the difficulties in voir dire of prospective jurors. He posed the hypo: it is a simple automobile accident case, but the client will appear to be effeminate, and his lawyer wants to peremptorily challenge persons who may vote against him because of that appearance. The professor's question to the students: how do you phrase the inquiry to the juror in such a manner that it will not offend any of the jury panel? One student's instant response: "why not ask him if he's ever been rear ended?" It was a while before the class was restored to order.

6. There Were Practical Jokes

Judge Bob Brinkman of Opelousas contributes this great story:

It was about ten o'clock on a Friday night in the old LSU law lounge. The usual crowd was there.

The discussion soon centered on Russia's testing of hydrogen bombs and the cumulative effect of radioactive fallout. "What's going to happen to us with all of the radioactive fallout?", someone asked. "Yea, what about all of the unborn children?", someone else intoned.

Dennis Whalen then proposed a solution. He suggested that if all young women of child bearing age were to get pregnant then, they could avoid bearing mutated fetuses. Thus was born the Society for the Transmission of Unmutated Descendants a/k/a S.T.U.D.

We then began drafting our proposition to all young maidens of child-bearing age. It was contained on a single sheet of paper. At the top was a baby with two heads, one leg and three arms. (I was the artist). The sketch was captioned: "This could be your child." The proposition followed: S.T.U.D. appreciated their plight but we offered a solution: if a young maiden became pregnant now before the Spring rain brought the fallout, she could avoid bearing a mutated child. Of course, S.T.U.D. offered its services at no cost to the young maidens.

Several hundred copies of the propositions were made by Ed Abell on the Law Institute's mimeograph machine – the old hand-crank kind. The copies were then promptly dispatched by S.T.U.D. members to the several women's dorms on the LSU campus.

Needless to say, something hit the fan!

It appears that the sensibilities of some genteel ladies (not the students, but their mothers) were offended. This prompted Dean French, the Dean of Men on the LSU campus, to begin an investigation into S.T.U.D. He hired two private detectives. The investigation was not really necessary, because there was no secret as to the identity of the S.T.U.D. members.

However, Dean Hebert was not going to let his law students be put on the sacrificial altar. He made a trip across campus, and the furor soon died.

Paul Harvey mentioned S.T.U.D. during one of his news broadcasts. Copies of campus newspapers from a California school and from the University of North Carolina informed that branch chapters of S.T.U.D. had been formed on those two campuses. The North Carolina newspaper suggested that those who were not accepted into S.T.U.D. should perform as free-lance operators.

In the 1950s the LSU Law student body occupied a special section in the student section at the LSU football games. Law School seniors generally attended clad in coat, tie, derby hat and cane. At one time, the Law Student section was adjacent to the section assigned to the LSU band. The combination of spirits and canes eventually produced "mini-battles" between the LSU seniors and band members, who did not take kindly to "cane prodding." However, the worst was yet to come. One law student found his way from the seating section to the floor of the stadium, where, using his cane as a "foil," he routed the head cheerleader, seized the field microphone, and proceeded to lead his fellow students in cheers, some of which could easily be deemed inappropriate in almost any circle. The student was quickly detained by police, but the episode was not over. On Monday morning, authorities were faced with the issue of the appropriate punishment for the recalcitrant law school senior. Expulsion was the punishment of choice by the "cross campus" authorities (the LSU Law Center was then a branch of the Baton Rouge campus). Dean Hebert pled for a lesser sentence, reminding the president of the university in a letter that the student "was training to enter a profession which was not known for its sobriety." Rumor has it that the ultimate punishment was that the law senior was allowed to continue and graduate, but that he was restricted in his movements on the LSU campus to a direct route of ingress and egress to the law building.

One professor learned a basic truth: it is futile to take oneself seriously when those around you do not. In the mid-1950s, this professor fell out of favor with a significant group of students. However, because of the limited number of offerings, many of them were required to take several courses with the professor. During one such course, before class began a member wrote on the blackboard: "Professor _____ is a fink." The professor, arriving a few minutes later, demanded to know who had written the words. No one responded, some because they feared retaliation by their classmates, and others because they subscribed to the same sentiment about the professor. The professor then admonished the class that if the professor learned who had written the words, that person's legal career would be aborted, but that until such time, the professor would not worry about it, because "anyone who criticizes another publicly but refuses to reveal his or her identity is a 'moral coward'." Two days later, the class met again, and there on the blackboard was written these words: "Professor _____ is still a fink. The moral coward strikes again!" As one might suspect, comments attributed to the "moral coward" appeared somewhere in the law school almost every day of that academic year.

7. But Some Jokes Were Not So Practical

In the 50s and 60s, the premier practical joke was to "fix up" a student with a date with a married woman, and then have the "husband" arrive and threaten violence. The scenario fell from favor when a student was killed accidentally (a fall while fleeing the "irate husband"). However, we have received at least a half dozen reports of "irate husband" scares (sometimes called the "Yellow Dog" trick) at the LSU Law School. Here is one of the best:

> For several weeks, Student "K" tells Student "H" that he has been dating a beautiful, scrumptious, young woman. Finally, "H" begs "K" to arrange a date with her. After several days of begging, "K" reluctantly agrees. The night of the date, "H" has taken a shower in preparation for his date and calls "K" to his room to ask him if the red polka dot shorts he is wearing would be appropriate. They then proceed to the apartment of the young woman and

"H" knocks on the door. Suddenly Student "S" (a large LSU athlete) emerges, points a 12 gauge shot gun at "H" and "K" and yells, "So, you are the S.O.B.s that have been dating my wife." "S" then leads "H" and "K" to the banks of the Mississippi with the shot gun pointed at them, with their hands raised up in the air. Suddenly "K" grabs the gun and begins struggling with "S" and yells, "run, H, run." And run he did. When he arrived at the law school dormitory, "H" was sweating profusely and was extremely afraid and worried. Then "K" walks in and says, "I think I killed him." "H," in a panic, says, "Am I an accomplice?" (We are in the midst of our course in Criminal Law with Professor Dale Bennett.)

"H" is extremely pale in color, wide-eyed, and in a frantic state. Suddenly, in walks "S" and everyone begins laughing. A very relieved "H" gives "S" a big hug.

Joe Koury
Lafayette

The practical joke was the order of the day at the LSU Law School in the 1950s. It was replaced in the 1960s by mythical awards to certain students, such as the "Better Living Through Chemistry" award to a student who was suspected of using (or overusing) drugs, and the "Whiplash" award to the female student most likely to turn the heads of male students as she walked past. One of the premier jokes did not involve sex, but a law student's other favorite quest – food. Near the end of a school year, after many of his classmates had fallen victims, one student (we'll call him Jay) announced emphatically that they'd never get him to fall for any joke. Immediately, putting one over on Jay became a class project. The ringleader in the project (we'll call him Chuck) was Jay's roommate. At that time, Bob and Jake's was a popular Baton Rouge restaurant which few law students could afford. Thus Jay was surprised when he received a letter on Bob and Jake's stationery addressed to him and advising him that Bob & Jake's was initiating a "get acquainted with the students" program through which they invited a student and his or her date or spouse to be their guests for dinner, and that Jay had been elected as guest number 6 for a particular week. When Jay told him about the letter, Chuck immediately warned Jay that it could be a practical joke. Nothing was said for a few days (the word was out among the students that the bait had been dangled before the "fish"). Then Chuck casually mentioned to Jay that a bigger joke would be if the letter were true, but that Jay passed up an expensive free meal because he was afraid of being tricked by his classmates. Chuck had an immediate solution: call Bob & Jake's and verify the offer. To assist Jay, Chuck grabbed a telephone directory, turned to the Bs, and read off what he represented to be Bob & Jake's number. In reality, it was the number of the apartment of a classmate; the classmate and his spouse had been answering the phone "Bob & Jake's" for several days. The respondent assured Jay that he was number 6 for the particular week. Since the now hooked "fish" had neither spouse nor date, he invited his roommate (Chuck) to accompany him. They feasted regally (the total bill was reputed to be $26, which was about one-fourth of a student's monthly income in those days) and when presented with the bill, Jay presented his letter. The manager's response was "Son, you've been had." His roommate did not reveal his participation in the activity (and may not yet have done so) and did not contribute to payment of the bill. The perpetrators allegedly had a greater scheme in mind (a call to the police by Bob and Jake's telling them they had caught a person attempting a scam, and a call to Bob and Jake's from the police warning them against such a possible scam), but abandoned that scheme when they realized that it could have repercussions beyond the law school.

Charlie Palmer of Amite submits this prank:

> Dickie Talbot and I turned up a bottle of disappearing ink, but after some nefarious searching for uses, we were handed a 'great" one on a silver platter the night Phil (later Judge) Savoie, wearing a white jacket, was leaving the Law Dorm for a date with the Darling of LSU.

> Talbot chased me down the law dorm stairs and as we ran by Phil, Talbot slashed/swished the disappearing

ink, dropping splotches of black ink across my shirt – BUT ALSO across Savoie's immaculate white jacket. When Phil looked at his coat, his urge was to do us in. Some new swearing epithets issued forth from him as we collapsed (with the others) in laughter. A few minutes later, at our behest, Phil looked down and sheepishly admitted "no harm" was done to his white jacket. (The ink had vanished.)

One observer of our prank (we'll call him Will) was so delighted with the Savoie incident he wanted to pull it on the Dekes (whose fraternity house was located across the street from the Law Dorm). However, instead of giving him disappearing ink, we gave him a bottle of permanent black ink.

At the DKE house, Will merrily splashed the ink over several Dekes and a campus queen who was there campaigning for co-ed vice-president. Some of the Dekes wanted to lynch Will, but he convinced them that the ink would disappear. After the passage of a period of time, it dawned on him that it was real ink. At that point, he managed somehow to slip out the back kitchen door, and was not seen around the DKE house for quite a while.

8. Some of The Fish Were Very Big

In the 1950s Dean Hebert was returning to law practice, and the president of the LSU system was looking for his replacement as dean of the law school. Some prankster students began circulating the rumor that the president was thinking about selecting a senior law student, sending him off for advanced training, and installing him as dean, i.e. a professional administrator. After the rumor had spread fully, the pranksters wrote a letter to one of the top academic seniors and a Law Review Editor on "President of LSU" stationery, inviting him to meet with the president to interview for the deanship. Not realizing that both of his legs were being pulled, the law student promptly appeared at the president's office and announced to the secretary that he was there to interview for the dean of the law school position. When the secretary looked quizzically at him, he showed her the letter. She looked at the initials at the bottom and said, "I type all of his letters and I did not type that one." Needless to say, he did not get the appointment.

9. But We Could Pull Together When We Had To

In the fifties, one of the students at the LSU Law School was employed at a neighborhood grocery store. At that time, gambling through football cards was a popular pastime. If one selected a number of winners (and, in some cases, beat the "point spread"), one was "rewarded" in cash. Picking 10 of 10 winners was a rarity, but it brought a hefty "reward" – as much as 100 to 1. The grocery at which the law student worked took bets on football cards, and the law student spent much time studying the regular players. One was an elderly gentleman who selected 10 potential winners each week – and never came close to winning. One Friday football weekend, the law student came up with an idea for supplemental pay – he would "book" the old gentleman's bet himself, and pocket the $1 (which, in those days, was not an insignificant amount). By Saturday afternoon, our law student was stunned to see that the card he was "booking" had nine of ten winners, with only the LSU Saturday night selection remaining. Unless LSU lost, the student was facing financial ruin and perhaps the end of a budding career in the law. He relayed his concerns to his classmates, who rallied behind him in the only way they knew how. That explains why at one Saturday night game, the entire LSU Law School section (in those days they sat together, the seniors adorned with hats and canes) cheered for LSU's opponent. Whether it was their cheers or fate, LSU lost and what was to become an outstanding legal career was rescued.

CHAPTER III

THE YOUNG LAWYER

1. Hustling For Business

Iddo Pittman of Hammond tells this story about his younger days:

It was April Fool's Day in 1949. My office was next door to a dentist. I had no secretary or receptionist and very few clients. Each day I hoped for a new client, but most days I was disappointed.

In the middle of the morning I received a telephone call from a rather nervous man telling me that he had been involved in an automobile accident near the Red Top Café, and that he needed a lawyer badly and he asked me to come to the scene of the accident and represent him.

I faced quite a dilemma. I was aware that it was April Fool's Day and I was also aware that I had many friends who would enjoy a joke, but I also badly needed the new client, so I took the risk and went to the alleged accident site.

Of course there was no accident and of course when I returned the dentist was waiting and he laughed and laughed and laughed. Not only did he laugh that day, but every April Fool's Day during the remainder of his lifetime, I received a similar phone call requesting that I come to the Red Top Café.

2. Here are some of the "gaffs" of the young and enthusiastic.

A young lawyer was late for criminal court. Upon his arrival, I expected him to express a reason for being late or maybe even an apology, so I asked him if he had any explanation for being late that he would care to share with me. His response, which I now consider to be a classic, was "It's because, your honor, I just got here".

Judge James E. Clark
Shreveport

Judge Jimmie C. Peters of Jena relates this tale:

I once was supplied with a classic example of the basic rule that before you say anything, you should know your audience. Appellate judges seldom have to dress the part, and my Jena office is very casual. On this particular day, I walked over to the courthouse for some reason long forgotten (the court house is across the street from my office). A jury trial was in recess, and a number of attorneys involved in the trial were standing on the steps of the court house. I only recognized one of the attorneys – an Alexandria practitioner whom I had known for several years. I stopped to visit for a moment. In the conversation he mentioned that during trial he had applied for and received a decision on an emergency writ to the Third Circuit. Before anything else could be said, a young attorney standing close by commented: "Yes, and the Third Circuit was wrong." I turned and, without changing expression, said, "No, the Third Circuit wasn't wrong." The Alexandria attorney was having difficulty keeping a straight face when the young lawyer, with a puzzled look on his face, continued with something to the effect that, "Not only was the Third Circuit wrong, but it was a stupid decision." Again, without changing expression, I stuck my hand out to the young lawyer and said, "Allow me to introduce myself. I am Judge Peters of the Third Circuit, and the Third Circuit is rarely wrong." The young man turned many indescribable shades of red, but as I walked away he had the perfect response. "Well, Judge," he said, "now I know what shoe leather tastes like."

3. Kids and Young Lawyers Say and Do the Darndest Things

A plaintiff lawyer may attempt to acclimate a jury toward large awards by emphasizing that the case before them is a "big one" because he or she only handles big cases. Here are a couple of times that strategy backfired.

> The jury was impaneled in the personal injury suit and it was time for opening statements. The plaintiff was represented by a flamboyant attorney who had a high opinion of his influence with juries drawn from the rural population of the district.
>
> Plaintiff's attorney went through the usual "boilerplate" language of an opening statement but before sitting down, he summarized with these remarks: "The one thing that you must keep in mind is that this is a BIG case. You know how to tell? Well, you all know me, and I can assure you that I only handle big cases."
>
> With that, he took a seat, and the young out-of-town defense lawyer stood before the panel and began with these remarks: "None of you know me. I am the junior member of a firm. And I can assure you that my firm only lets me try little cases."
>
> Judge Ward Fontenot
> Cameron

A young lawyer was faced with a similar argument, i.e., the case was a "big" one because the older plaintiff lawyer only handled big cases. The young lawyer began her opening argument by exhibiting to the jury a copy of her firm's letterhead, pointing out the position of her name at the end of a long list of attorneys, and asking: "Do you think my firm would let anybody this far down the line try a big case"?"

A young lawyer was trying an important case in front of a

visiting judge he did not know. After the case was taken under advisement, the lawyer purchased a big box of candy and a fine bottle of wine and placed them on the secretary's desk in the visiting judge's chambers; neither visiting judge nor secretary was there at the time. Shortly thereafter, the young lawyer was telling several attorney friends about the a case and about the judicial "gift." One senior lawyer reacted strongly, telling the young lawyer he had made a huge mistake and that the visiting judge would not tolerate such blatant conduct. The young lawyer looked startled, left quickly and returned a few minutes later with a smile and a look of relief on his face. The senior attorney asked the young lawyer if he had been able to retrieve the ill-advised "gift." "No," he responded, "but I got there in time to change the name on the card."

A young lawyer was in what was obviously his first "first chair" (if not his first "any chair") trial and his inexperience was showing. However, little harm was anticipated because it was a bench trial and the young lawyer's client had been rear-ended by another vehicle while stopped at a red light. At the close of the evidence, a slightly more experienced defense counsel moved for a directed verdict. The judge looked at the empty jury box, shrugged her shoulders, and said: "Obviously you mean a motion to dismiss and I'll so treat it. Let's hear your argument." Defense counsel then made a brief argument that there was no proof of any negligence in the record. The judge overruled the objection on that basis, reminding defense counsel that she was defending a rear-ending motorist, but then said, "I'll sustain your motion on the basis that the defendant made a general denial and there is no evidence in the record that the defendant was driving the rear-ending vehicle." Plaintiff counsel stood, looked at the judge, looked at defense counsel, and then back at the judge, swallowing hard for what must have been 30 seconds. Finally, the judge asked, "Would you like some help?" "Yes," cried plaintiff counsel, now near the fainting stage. "Well," said the court, "move for it." Again counsel thought for a moment, swallowed hard, and blurted out, "I move for help." The judge treated it as a motion to reopen, and the day was saved.

4.   If You Ask A Stupid Question

A young attorney was handling probably his first confirmation of default. His attire was immaculately court proper, his court manners were distinguished, and his questions succinctly to the point. His young woman client had filed for a legal separation from her husband on the grounds of cruel treatment. She was about 21 years and a beautiful blonde, and she was wearing a simple, inexpensive dress, but one which seemed to amplify attributes of the physique it purported to hide. Every male in the courtroom (including the judge) observed and admired her as she approached the bench, each of us thinking: "Some guy fouled up terribly."

> Attorney (after certain preliminary offerings): "And he often accuses you of having sexual relations with other men. Is that true?"
>
> Lovely One: "Yes."
>
> Attorney: "And those accusations are not true, are they?"
>
> Lovely One: "Not always."

The young attorney quickly moved on to the next question, hoping that the judge was asleep. (I was not, but I did not question the witness and granted the separation).

Judge Paul Newell
Minden

A private detective testified that after observing the suspect wife and a man leave a bar and get into a car, he observed their silhouettes, embracing and kissing in the darkened car, and that after a while all he could see was a pair of feet on the dashboard. The husband's young lawyer asked, "Could you tell if they were male or female feet?" (I had to leave the bench).

Judge Tony Graphia
Baton Rouge

5. Knowing When To Fold 'Em

I have always told our young lawyers to shut up when they are ahead in a trial, but some never learn. One time I was in a multi-sided civil case with a lawyer from Baton Rouge. He was a fine fellow and a very capable lawyer, but he never knew when to shut up. We were representing co-defendants, and he had filed some motions or exceptions which were unquestionably good. When the case was called for hearing, the judge addressed him and told him that he had read the exceptions and they seemed well founded. This fellow just had to have his say and present his well-prepared argument, however, so he stood and started to talk. After about five minutes, the irritated judge pounded the bench with his gavel and said, "Mr. _____, after hearing your argument I have become convinced that my original judgment was wrong. Exception overruled." Of course, the lawyer's client eventually was properly dismissed from the case.

Howard Gist
Alexandria

6. Living With the Senior Partner

A young lawyer was assigned a minor misdemeanor trial which the senior partner viewed as a certain loser but a good learning experience for the novice. Surprisingly, the young lawyer prevailed and upon returning to the office the senior asked about the result. The young lawyer said proudly, "justice prevailed," to which the senior promptly responded, "Don't take it lying down, appeal immediately."

Every young lawyer is in awe of at least one of his senior partners. One of the authors shares this episode from his early beginnings:

When I joined Booth, Lockard, Jack, Pleasant & LeSage in February 1959, I was the only associate for five hard working trial lawyers. They kept me busy in the library, securing information and checking evidence, witnesses, and potential jurors. Necessarily, the matters in trial, or closest to trial, got priority. That worked with everybody except Mr. Lockard, who apparently thought that everything I was working on for him, except for Mr. Harry Booth's assignments, should be first. My office was across and a bit down the hall from the partners. One morning I heard Mr. Lockard coming down the hall jingling the change in his pocket as was his wont, and I knew he was going to ask for a status report on an auto accident he had told me to investigate a couple of days before. I had not had an opportunity to do anything except to get a police accident report. I didn't want to have to explain to the "Big L," as we affectionately called Mr. Lockard, that more pressing matters consumed me, so I told my secretary to tell him I was out. I then dropped down on all fours and hid behind my desk as he came in, glanced in my office and, seeing nothing, asked my secretary where I was. Incapable of telling a bald-faced lie, my secretary said, "Isn't he in his office?" When the Big L said "No," she continued, "Apparently he stepped out for a few minutes." I breathed a sigh of relief, but then the phone rang and our operator called over the office intercom system, "Mr. Lockard, line 2 for you." To my dismay he said, "I'll take it in Hank's office." I had little choice but to back myself under my desk. Usually the Big L was very concise and quick on telephone calls, but he could not end this one from his doctor client so easily. He decided to come around my desk and sit in my chair to continue the conversation. I pushed even further back, with only my head, hands, feet, and knees visible. As he concluded the telephone call, he looked down at me and said, "I thought you were out." I could not say anything. He immediately stood up, exited my office, and went into the stairwell to go downstairs from our second-story office suite.

I dragged myself out from under my desk and went in to tell Mr. Harry what I had done; I stood ready to offer my resignation. He listened attentively as I related the above and said, "We know that Leonard has little patience and is very demanding of you. We are all very pleased with your work." Then he asked if I had finished gathering the evidence we needed for an expropriation case involving property near Arcadia for then-under-construction I-20. I told him that I had everything except certain photos, but a photographer was ready to meet me there whenever we asked. He told me to take his car and go immediately to Arcadia, but to leave the building from the rear exit because Mr. Lockard was next door having a cup of coffee with a friend. I did as I was told, and returned late that afternoon and brought Mr. Harry his car. He simply told me that I still had my job and that the Big L would never ever mention the matter to me. He was right.

It was not until years later that I pressed Mr. Harry to tell me the rest of the story. A few minutes after I eased out the rear of the building and drove off to Arcadia in Mr. Harry's car, the Big L came into his office saying, "Harry, we've got to talk about this Politz boy. He seems bright, he works hard, he never complains, but the boy troubles me, Harry." Mr. Harry responded, "In what way," whereupon the Big L said: "A little while ago I went into his office to take a telephone call. I was told he was out of the office but he wasn't, Harry. He was squeezed up like a little puppy under his desk." Mr. Harry told me that he paused and looked at Big L and then said slowly: "Leonard, I sent Hank to Arcadia early this morning on that expropriation case we have over there. He is to meet the photographer and complete our investigation. He won't be back until late this afternoon, and he has my car so I would like a ride home with you." At that point the Big L slapped his wrist where he had a band-aid and said, "Damn it, I told my doctor that the new medicine he was giving me was causing me to hallucinate."

Bill Jarman of Baton Rouge submits this story:

> As a young lawyer with the firm then known as Sanders, Downing, Kean and Cazedessus in Baton Rouge, I was representing the State in a medical malpractice case brought by an Angola inmate. When it was time to argue, the inmate (representing himself) shuffled up to the table in his orange coveralls; his feet were chained together and he was holding a ball weight. When he reached counsel table, he grabbed his left wrist with his right hand and pulled his entire left arm out of his sleeve – it was a prosthesis and his medical treatment regarding the missing left limb was the subject of his medical malpractice suit. I made an argument on some nominal exception, the prisoner made his argument, and then Judge Alford, as he often did, said, "Mr. Jarman – you make some good points with your exception, but I am going to just refer it to the merits of the trial."
>
> I got up from the table with my briefcase and papers while the prisoner put his arm back on and gathered his ball and chain.
>
> As I was walking out of the back of the court room, my mentor and senior partner, Gordon Kean, stopped me. Kean had been in the back the whole time waiting to argue another rule. Kean looks me in the eye and says, "Damn, Jarman; you can't beat a one-armed man with his feet chained together?"

7. Living With the Judge

The late Chief Justice John Fournet was perhaps the world's greatest intimidator of young lawyers. One of his ploys (to which many of us fell victim, and later watched eagerly as other young lawyers had their turn) was to allow the young lawyer, obviously arguing in the high court for the first time, to begin his argument. The chief justice would be looking down, perhaps at a document on the bench, and would allow the young lawyer to proceed long enough to become comfortable and confident. At the proper moment, the Chief Justice would look up, with a scowl on his face, and ask gruffly, "Who're you?" There is no known case of a young lawyer's knees not buckling at that moment.

However, Paul Deal of New Orleans relates the tale long circulated about Fournet and the young lawyer who had his first case before the Louisiana Supreme Court. It seems that the lawyer was arguing at great length and the Court was unusually quiet. Finally, Chief Justice Fournet is said to have held up his hand to stop the lawyer from speaking, and to have said in essence, "Young man, I have been listening to you attentively for the last 20 minutes and I am no wiser that I was when you started." Whereupon the young lawyer replied, "Yes, Mr. Chief Justice, but you are now much better informed."

Another Fournet story comes to us from Bruce Rozas of Mamou:

> Following graduation from LSU in 1968, I clerked for a year for the Honorable J. Cleveland Fruge of the Third Circuit in Lake Charles. Judge Fruge was very close to his law clerks and called them all his "sons"; I was No. 9. Likewise, he was always trying to help us advance our careers. Soon after my clerkship ended, I attended my first Bar Association convention in Mississippi and, being a young lawyer from the rural part of the state, I knew very few of the older lawyers or judges attending the convention. Judge Fruge took every opportunity to introduce me to important lawyers and to every judge that we came upon. At that time I still smoked, and one afternoon I was standing near the judge in a large crowd. We finished our conversation and, before putting out a cigarette, I took a last "draw" on it, filling my lungs with smoke just as Supreme Court Chief Justice Fournet walked up to Judge Fruge. The judge turned quickly to introduce me to the Chief and I found myself facing the Chief with lungs full of smoke. The Chief immediately stuck out his hand and I did the same, not wanting to delay a second, but when I tried to speak a huge cloud of smoke erupted from my mouth and covered the Chief to

the point that we could no longer see each other through the haze. He took his other hand and tried to find me in the smoke and said in his usual impressive voice – "Son, you must be on fire!" Needless to say, the introduction was an embarrassment to me and the Judge, who simply looked at me and said: "You should stop that!" I met the Chief on a few other occasions before he retired and fortunately he either didn't remember or graciously never mentioned it, and neither did Judge Fruge.

8. The Things They Don't Teach You In Law School

Richard Edrington of Laplace shares this "jewel":

A contemporary of mine, a recent admittee to the Bar in the late 60s and early 70s, was in Civil District Court confirming a default in a divorce matter. In those days, of course, the Soldiers and Sailors Civil Relief Act required a person confirming a default to provide an affidavit attesting that the defaulted defendant was not in military service. My young contemporary put on the evidence to confirm the default, and then was asked to make his offer. He proceeded to introduce the entire record to indicate the date of service and the date the preliminary default was entered. The judge then asked the lawyer whether he had his non-military affidavit. Not knowing what one was, and not having been told what one was, or that he needed it, and being extremely quick on his feet, the lawyer proceeded to advise the Court that he was not aware that he would need such a thing that day, but he wanted to assure His Honor that he had been honorably discharged from the United States Marine Corps in 1964!

9. Advice to the Young Lawyer

Since time immemorial, the younger generation has displaced the older one, usually before the older one was ready to be sent out to pasture. Not so in the law, however. While the younger lawyer has his youth and a better education, the old pro has seen it all at least once. So our advice to young lawyers: don't ever underestimate your opponent, even though he walks slowly, snoozes often, and practices in a country town you've never heard of. A sign which hung in the office of the late Phillip Saal of Gueydan sums it up: "Age and Treachery will always overcome Youth and Skill."

10. The Worst of All Possible Whirls

Perhaps the most "flabbergasted" young lawyer was the one flying to Atlanta to argue before the Fifth Circuit prior to the split into the Fifth and Eleventh Circuits. The young lawyer was reviewing documents as the plane proceeded toward Atlanta. Sitting next to him was a man learned in the law but not displaying it. He asked the young lawyer: "Are you a lawyer." Upon receiving an affirmative response, he then queried: "What are you getting ready for?" The young lawyer then told him that he was going to argue a case in the U.S. Fifth Circuit, that it was one of the most prestigious opportunities a young lawyer could have, and that only important young lawyers got a chance to do so. The young lawyer then asked his questioner: "What do you do for a living?" "Well," said the questioner, "I work for the government; I occasion people to stand up and sit down in court." The young lawyer said, "Oh, you're a bailiff," and the conversation tailed off. The next morning, as the court was announced and entered the courtroom, the young attorney was stunned when he saw that his questioner on the airplane the previous day was the co-author hereof, Hank Politz, then a judge (and later chief judge) of the Fifth Circuit. As did all counsel, the attorney stood up and sat down, muttering under his breath words which sounded like "occasion people to stand up and sit down, like hell." He recovered sufficiently to argue his case, doing quite well, but avoiding eye contact with one member of the panel.

CHAPTER IV

CLIENTS ARE PEOPLE,
AND PEOPLE ARE FUNNY

A client usually is a person who has a problem but little or no knowledge of how the law operates. That combination produces some strange stories. A favorite comes from Judge E. L. (Bubba) Guidry of St. Martinville.

> One day, while I was serving as a district judge, I received a call from a woman who proceeded to tell me the story of her troubles. When she paused long enough for me to get a word in, I said, "Mrs. Boudreaux, you should see a lawyer." "Well," she said, "I've got a lawyer but he ain't doing me no good. What I need is a judge."

J. D. Cascio of Monroe reports a strange client inquiry:

> A lady telephoned late one Saturday night. I had already gone to bed. My wife answered the phone, and as she was handing me the receiver she told me that the caller wanted to speak to the lawyer Cascio. I was barely awake when I took the receiver and said, "Hello." As soon as I did the caller, in an excited voice, proceeded to tell me that she had left her husband because of the cruel way he had been treating her; that she had been hiding from him for a couple of weeks; that he had just telephoned her and told her that he knew where she was, and that he was going to come over and kill her. She then asked: "Can he do that?" (I wanted to reply: "No Ma'am, but if he does you call me back.)" But now being fully awake, I demurred and gave her the needed advice.

Howard Gist of Alexandria provides this vignette of Louisiana life:

> My father loved to tell a funny tale about a land

sale in which he represented the seller. This was supposed to be a cash sale for what was then a rather substantial sum of money. The buyers were immigrants who had come to Louisiana from Europe by way of Chicago, and were members of a large group who were enticed to come to Louisiana after being induced to purchase poor lands north of the Red River. These people were honest and industrious; they settled there and, despite all odds, made a good living, but they were very unpretentious.

The buyers, an elderly man and wife, came to Daddy's office rather poorly dressed, to say the least. When it came time to pay the money, they started counting out old and dirty bills in various denominations. They came up short. Dad says that the old man looked at the old lady and said, "Ma, we must have dug up the wrong can." They must have, because they left and shortly returned with enough money to close the deal.

John Lanier of Thibodaux learned the true meaning of "Hell hath no fury like a woman scorned." He was appointed by the court to inventory the property of a couple involved in a separation proceeding. It was a bitter battle between husband and wife, neither willing to relinquish any claims to any property which they owned. On the appointed day, the two appraisers and John arrived at the family home for the inventory. The wife, who occupied the home, met them at the door with fire in her eyes. She was suspicious and belligerent to the point that John had to tell her that if she didn't quit fussing and interfering with their taking of the inventory, he would have to ask the judge to hold her in contempt.

She insisted that they list everything – every pot and pan, plate, glass, knife, fork, spoon, salt shaker, even the rolls of toilet paper. When the appraisal team was in the bedroom, she insisted that they list the contents of her sewing basket, so they listed every needle, pin, thimble and spool of thread.

John and the appraisers endured this as they went through the house, room by room. After hours of aggravation, it appeared that they finally had finished the task. They had inventoried everything in the house, and had even counted the chickens and animals in the yard.

As they prepared to leave, the disgruntled wife called to them and said, "Wait, you forgot one thing. You see that chicken coop in the backyard. I want my husband to get his share of everything that is in it." It was empty, of course, except for the chicken droppings on the floor!

Michael Bordelon of Mandeville discovered some interesting layperson perceptions while serving as a young lease broker in rural Livingston Parish. Here are a couple of his experiences.

1.   The oil company was initially offering a 1/6th royalty (along with the lease payment) so when preparing the lease, I would routinely change the preprinted 1/8th royalty to the tendered 1/6th. One landowner accused me of "screwing" him when he saw the change because he was no fool, he knew that "8 was bigger than 6."

2.   I was making my pitch to obtain a mineral lease from a small landowner. After explaining the exploration and leasing process, royalty, drilling and surface rights, and especially what could happen if the landowner didn't lease or "rode the well down," I told the landowner that the lease payment was $100 per acre. The offer was considered for some time and finally the landowner took out his checkbook and began writing a check. Apparently, he thought that he had to pay to get a well drilled. When I told him that he was not to pay, that they would get paid, he lit up like a Madame LaRue pinball machine.

Stan Bardwell of Baton Rouge tells this story of an unusual will signing.

A statutory will requires that the testator declare in the presence of the Notary and the witnesses that the document in question is, and is understood by the testator to be, his or her will. My standard practice is to assemble everyone involved, make appropriate introductions, then utter the formula question, "Now, Mr./Mrs. Testator, is this your last will and testament which you wish to sign in the presence of these witnesses?", or words to that effect. The universal answer has been a simple "Yes". Recently, I went through the litany, "Is this your Last Will and Testament?", to which the old gentleman said, "Well, I certainly hope so!"

We're all familiar with "self help" testators, i.e., those who make or amend their wills without legal advice. Robert Dunkelman of Shreveport reports one such event:

> During my first week as a lawyer in Shreveport, I was asked by Joe Milner, a senior partner in the firm and one whose reputation for legal ability and professionalism was beyond reproach, to "walk through" the probate documents on an olographic testament. All of the pleadings had been prepared by Mr. Milner and appeared to be in order. I reviewed the will, and it satisfied all of the formalities for an olographic testament (i.e. it was entirely written, dated and signed in the testator's handwriting).

> The testator, however, had added an additional formal requirement of his own. The testator apparently believed that a will must be contained on the front of one 8 ½ x 11 piece of paper. Accordingly, the handwriting grew smaller and smaller toward the bottom of the page. The testament was, nonetheless, signed in the bottom right-hand corner by the testator.

> This particular day, the "order signing" judge at Caddo District Court was Chief Judge C. J. Bolin. I went to his office and was greeted by Judge Bolin. A pleasant conversation ensued about his grandchildren, my background, etc. Judge Bolin then reviewed all of the documents which had been prepared by Mr. Milner, and

they all appeared to be in order. Judge Bolin then read the will, and it appeared to be in order. Then Judge Bolin took out his *ne varietur* stamp and stamped the top of the will and signed his name thereto. This is where the problem began.

Because of the density of the handwriting at the bottom of the page, Judge Bolin struggled to find a place at the conclusion of the will on which to affix his *ne varietur* stamp. The only possible location for the stamp was on the bottom left-hand corner of the will. As the stamp approached the paper, Judge Bolin said "what is this?" We then both closely examined the bottom left-hand portion of the paper, and discovered to our surprise that that portion of the will had liquid paper on it.

It was an incredible job of liquid papering – absolutely undetectable to cursory examination. The cover-up would have gone undetected if there had been another place for Judge Bolin to affix the *ne varietur* stamp.

Judge Bolin and I then proceeded to his bathroom where we could read through the back of the paper, using the bright lights and bathroom mirror to assist in our interpretation. Needless to say, there was nothing attached.

"We've got a problem," Judge Bolin said, as I started wondering what the world record was for the shortest time between admission to the bar and disbarment. We then went to the foyer where the incredible liquid paper job was shown to other members of the bench. To this day, I try to believe that the comments that were made in the foyer were just light-hearted banter. Needless to say, I was intensely paranoid at this juncture, and my recollection of the events in the foyer is probably tainted.

I was instructed by Judge Bolin to return to our offices (a block away) and to have Mr. Milner call Judge

Bolin upon my arrival. When I arrived, I found that Mr. Milner already was talking on the phone with Judge Bolin. Most of the conversation seemed to center on the "Rembrandt" of a liquid paper job on the bottom of that will and on how funny it was that a "rookie" had been sent to probate it.

As it played out, after the will had been executed the testator and his wife, an elderly couple, had added a codicil to leave their children specific items of personal belongings. As they aged, all of the items listed on the codicil were transferred to the children by donation *inter vivos*. After all of the codicil items had been disbursed, the codicil was destroyed and "Michelangelo" went to work on the bottom left corner of the 8 ½ x 11 sheet of paper. Since that time, I have personally loathed Michael Nesmith's mother for the invention of liquid paper, and have only handled one other succession-related matter (a pro bono for my family).

Alan Fishbein of Baton Rouge provides this story:

A divorce client was advised by her counsel that she could not engage in sexual relations until the divorce was completed. The female looked at counsel with surprise and shock and said "I would never do anything like that." Two weeks later, opposing counsel called her attorney and said they had caught her at a particular motel, that she had checked in with a male friend at a certain time, and did not leave until the next morning at approximately 9:00 a.m. Her counsel called the client into his office and asked whether she had committed adultery. Her reply was "of course not. I am a religious person and would not do that." Her counsel then told her about the call from opposing counsel and asked whether she thought the court would believe that they had played monopoly, she said, "No." When asked what she had done at the motel, she replied that she had engaged in oral sex with her friend, but that that was not adultery.

The following story probably is apocryphal (or it has occurred on several occasions). One version is that a routine alimony rule was being processed by one of Caddo Parish's senior trial judges. The husband was not represented by counsel and the facts were not complicated. The wife testified about her expenses and her limited income. The husband was asked about his work, income and assets. The judge moved quickly to resolution, addressing the parties but looking at the husband who was still in the witness box. "Alright now, I've heard the evidence and the court is going to give your wife $25 a week." The husband broke in with "Thank you judge, thank you, and if I gets able, from time to time I'll put something on her too." The judge quickly advised, "No, the court makes the award, you pay it." The husband responded in a hushed voice, "Oh, that do make a difference."

CHAPTER V

THE LAWYERS

1. Pleading

Lawyers take liberty with pleading, particularly where the stakes are low or the controversy is humorous. Our favorite comes from Judge Preston Aucoin of Ville Platte, who tells this story from his younger days.

> Once when I was a practicing lawyer, I defended a man who had been sued by a disgruntled lover for the return of $4,500 she had given him from her husband's community savings account to buy a car. Since I appreciated the law to be that once you have freely and voluntarily made a manual gift of a movable (including cash) you can't get it back, I filed an "Exception of Indian Giver." Incredibly, the trial judge, Joe LaHaye, did not hold me in contempt of court, and granted my exception.

Lloyd Bourgeois of Thibodaux tells this one.

> When a co-defendant filed a cross claim against my client alleging that his insured driver had been forced to leave his lane of travel because there was an alligator in his path, I filed an answer in which I denied the 'allegations and the alligator." From that day forward, Judge Pettigrew thought that I was more interested in sabotage than in practicing law.

2. Attendance Records

This case of the "tardy lawyer" has been around for a while. Two contributors identified him as Walter Dumas of Baton Rouge. Here is one version:

> Dumas did not arrive at the scheduled time; nevertheless, the judge began the trial without him. An hour or so into the trial, Dumas walked in. The judge

halted the matter in progress and greeted an ever cheerful Dumas with a sarcastic welcome that, "Well, Mr. Dumas. We are certainly glad you were able to join us for your case. We started without you," to which Walter is said to have replied, "Thank you, Judge. How am I doing?"

Stan Bardwell
Baton Rouge

3.   Lawyering and the Objection

The extemporaneous nature of the objection produces some interesting dialogue. Here are the best examples we've collected.

I was defending a municipality in a civil bench trial in St. Tammany Parish. The plaintiff, whose car had fallen in a hole within the road right-of-way, presented a witness to attest that the hole had been there for a long time. On cross-examination I began questioning the witness about the circumstances surrounding her alleged prior knowledge. As the witness's story began to unravel a bit, I began to use ever more leading questions. As the witness began to agree to things that were seemingly inconsistent with her testimony on direct examination, plaintiff's attorney jumped up and exclaimed, "Objection! Counsel is putting things in the witness's mind!" I stopped and looked at him, then turned to the judge, who had the same puzzled look on his face as I did, and asked, "Putting things in the witness's mind?" The judge then asked the plaintiff's attorney, "Counsel, what article of the Code of Evidence are you citing?" He responded with a simple, "Withdrawn."

Danny Garrett
Baton Rouge

I once had a claims adjuster on the stand testifying about a statement he had taken from the plaintiff to the effect that the plaintiff had not been involved in an accident on board my client's vessel. This statement included a line in which the plaintiff said that, when he woke up at 6:00 a.m. for shift change, his back was hurting, but he could not remember being involved in any accident. The plaintiff's attorney cross examined the adjuster by asking at what time the shift changed, and received the reply of "6:00 a.m." Accordingly, the plaintiff's counsel attacked the witness on the grounds that the statement must be incorrect because a crew going on duty at 6 a.m. certainly must have awakened prior to the moment of crew change. My witness replied "Aw, that's just splitting hairs." Judge Patrick Carr of the Eastern District of Louisiana admonished the witness that it was his job to answer questions. The witness apologized and asked the plaintiff's counsel to repeat the question. When he did so, I objected on the grounds that the question was "nit picking." Judge Carr then sustained my objection.

Hal Welch
New Orleans

Several years ago, I defended a Greek shipowner who was being sued by a Greek seaman injured while the vessel was docked in the port of New Orleans. Plaintiff's attorney, Paul Dué of Baton Rouge, associated Russ Herman of New Orleans, and the case was allotted to Judge Tom Early, Civil District Court for the Parish of Orleans.

The plaintiff had settled his workers' compensation claim against the shipowner with a general release of all claims. Based on the Zorgias case, an opinion authored by U.S. District Judge Alvin Rubin, I filed an exception of res judicata. The Zorgias case, which was decided on motion for summary judgment, relied on an affidavit by Professor Yiannopoulos, an expert on Greek law.

On the morning of the hearing, Paul Dué and Russ Herman brought Professor Yiannopoulos to the court room. I approached him and asked: "Yippy, what are you doing here?" He responded: "Don, I'm going to testify against you." I responded: "But my exception is based on the <u>Zorgias</u> case, which relied upon your affidavit." He responded: "The law has changed. There is a recent case from the Court in Piraeus. Here is a copy." I looked at it and exclaimed: "I can't read this. It's in Greek." He replied: "I shall interpret it for the Court."

When I moved for a continuance on the hearing of my exception, I told the Court, "I claim surprise. I was not advised that Professor Yiannopoulos would testify on a new case. I need time to have it translated and to obtain my own expert on Greek law."

Russ Herman responded: "Mr. Hoffman is no more surprised than ten guys at a stag party where a giant cake is brought into the room and out jumps a naked woman." I replied: "I'm as surprised as those guys would be if a naked Russ Herman jumped out of that cake. They would need time to prepare for what might happen next."

Judge Early, smiling, ruled: "I've got to grant your continuance based on the image alone." Several months later, after the matter was submitted, the exception of res judicata was granted and the case was dismissed.

Don Hoffman
New Orleans

One of the first trials in the Lafayette division of the United States District Court was in a cramped, temporary courtroom. Because of the lack of space, the young attorney who had prepared the case was required to sit behind his senior partner, who was trying the case. During the trial, the senior partner asked a question which the junior partner knew would lead to the introduction of harmful evidence. Junior partner jumped to his feet, and to the astonishment of senior partner, objected to the question, claiming that the answer would be irrelevant. While initially taken aback by the co-counsel's objection, the court denied it and the harmful response was admitted.

Bob Wright
Lafayette

When I first became district judge, I found that the transition from trial attorney to judge was more than expected. In one of my earliest contested hearings, one of the attorneys questioning a witness asked an obviously objectionable question. Forgetting that I was no longer an attorney, and being so intensely involved in listening to every word, I immediately said, "I object." The opposing attorney stood up and said, "Thank you, Your Honor. I do too."

Judge Jimmy Peters
Jena

An attorney defending a murder case in my court objected strenuously to the introduction of a piece of evidence and his objection was sustained. He then said, "Thank you, Your Honor, I would like to make a bill of exception." I said, "Mr. Blank, I sustained your objection." He said, "I know that, Your Honor, I would like to perfect my exception anyway." He did not believe he had done this until after the record was read to him.

Judge Richard Putnam
Abbeville

Mrs. Elodie Kidd Parker, one of the few Louisiana female attorneys in 1970, had a way of handling objecting attorneys. On my first day after being admitted to the Bar, my employers "threw me to the wolves" by sending me, without any advance warning, to court to try a rule against Ms. Parker. Unalerted, I sat next to her at the counsel table, and each time I stood to object (which was often), she placed her hand on my shoulder, shoved me back into my chair, and said something to the effect of, "Sit down, I'm not through yet!" When I looked to Judge Clyde Russell for assistance, he made it plain from the look on his face that he had no intention of entering into that fray, and that I was on my own. Thereafter, when in court with Ms. Elodie, I sat on the opposite side of the counsel table.

Judge Jimmie Peters
Jena

4. Questions, Questions

Justice Jeff Victory of Shreveport provides this story:

Back in the 1970s, Judge Charles Lindsay, who was then an assistant D.A. in Caddo Parish, was prosecuting a defendant for a felony. Five of the six jurors had been selected and another three member panel of prospective jurors was seated in the box for questioning.

Lindsay, as usual, questioned all the prospective jurors thoroughly before tendering them to a defense attorney, who was well known for his excessive consumption of alcohol. The defense attorney's total voir dire to all three prospective jurors consisted of the following:

To Prospective Juror #1

Lawyer:	"You say your name is Johnson?"
Juror:	"Yes."
Lawyer:	"I knew a fellow named Johnson once. He was a pretty nice guy. Judge, we'll take this one – you two fellows can hit the road."

Sometimes attorneys have difficulty asking the most simple questions. Note this exchange with a battered wife. "In what physical proximity were the injuries inflicted?" "What?" Please state the point of contact of the battery." "Sir?" The court intervened with "Where did your husband hit you?" The witness, relieved to understand the inquiry, responded, "Oh, your Honor, I was on the slop jar."·

Here is a short one on Burt Willis, who was bilingual and who was known for his courtroom eloquence, sprinkled with quotations from Shakespeare and the Bible.

Burt did not use depositions very much; somebody once remarked that to Burt "cross-examination was his favorite discovery device." One day he called on cross-examination a person who was dressed in khaki pants and a white shirt buttoned at the neck, but without a tie. Burt presumed that the witness was a working class Cajun, and asked him: "Vous parlez Anglais?" The man gave Burt a quizzical stare and did not reply. Burt repeated "Vous parlez Anglais" but again he got no response. Burt turned to the judge and said "Judge, I asked the man in French if he could speak English and he refuses to answer my question," at which point the witness said: "Oh, now I understand! I speak English. I don't speak French."

Smitty Landry
New Iberia

A Series of Prize Questions

Q: And you are how old a woman, sir?

Q: Now isn't it true that when a person dies in his sleep in most cases he just passes quietly away and doesn't know anything about it until the next morning?

Q.   Was it you or your brother that was killed in the war?

Q: And the youngest son, the 20-year-old, how old is he?

Q.   Were you alone or by yourself?

Q.   Were you present in the courtroom this morning when you were sworn in?

Q: Did you see it with your own eyes?

The defendant had committed what could only be described as a particularly stupid felonious act. The witness had shared a jail cell with the defendant for several years. An issue before the court was defendant's legal competence. After the customary scene setting questions, the following question and answer ensued:

Q.   What was your impression of his behavior and his psychological state at that time?

A.   Well, he had his lights on, but nobody was at home.

5.   Oral Argument

Guy D'Antonio was defending a Mr. Wong on bookmaking charges in Federal Court. Some of the government's evidence was obtained from a garbage can, so Guy filed a motion to suppress. At the subsequent hearing, he made his argument and, when finished, the government rebutted, citing the case of State v. White. When they were finished, Mr. D'Antonio looked at the Judge and said: "Your Honor, obviously the government doesn't know the difference between White and Wong." The Judge put his head down on his desk but could not contain his laughter.

Michael Bordelon
Mandeville

While clerking at the Second Circuit Court of Appeal, I witnessed one of the shortest oral arguments by an appellant's counsel. In this case the appellant was faced with adverse precedent from the Supreme Court of Louisiana directly on point. After reciting the facts in a sentence or two, appellant's seasoned attorney stated, "I'll be brief. I'm merely passing through on my way to the Supreme Court." He lost in the appellate court, and writs were denied.

Tom Richard
Southern University Law Center

The story oft repeated in the Fifth Circuit (but, I believe, is more accurately attributable to the Supreme Court of Texas) involves an incident at oral argument on a case that pitted proponents and opponents of elevating Odessa (Texas) Junior College to a full 4-year college. When counsel for the proponents of the increase was asked by a member of the appellate panel to explain the justification for establishing a 4-year college in Odessa, the barrister replied, "Your Honor, there is enough ignorance there to warrant an 8-year college!"

Judge Jacques Weiner
Shreveport

Charles Salley, Jimmy Johnson, John T. Campbell (Jimmy's senior partner) and I were trying a wrongful death case in Bossier Parish. Jimmy did most of the work for the plaintiff's side and gave the plaintiff's closing argument. Charles had a bad case. In his closing Charles suggested that the deceased, who was in his late sixties or early seventies, had a limited life expectancy and that the jury, should it award damages, should take that fact into consideration. John T., who was only about 5'5" in height, completely bald, and in his late eighties, got up to address the jury in rebuttal. He pushed his glasses back up on his head, placed his forearms on the rail of the jury box and, with his chin resting on his hands, said: "Ladies and Gentlemen, a man's life does not really begin until he's eighty."

Caldwell Roberts
Shreveport

Counsel for plaintiff was making what he obviously thought was a brilliant, thorough and detailed argument when he was interrupted by Judge Richard Putnam, who told him: "Counsel, my inclination was to deny defendant's motion, but if you keep talking, I may have to change my mind."

Bob Wright
Lafayette

A case was being argued to a Fifth Circuit Court of Appeals panel that included the legendary John Minor Wisdom. Judge Wisdom asked counsel at the podium, a well-known lawyer from Midland, Texas, "Counsel, are you familiar with the maxim inclusio unius est exclusio alterius?" Without hesitation, counsel responded sanctimoniously, "Your Honor, in Midland they speak of little else."

Judge Jacques Weiner
Shreveport

C. E. Laborde, Jr., was a long-time Avoyelles Parish attorney. On one occasion he found himself involved in a state tax assessment appeal, not too familiar territory for him. The appeal was heard by the State Tax Commission, whose members were appointed from around the state. One of those members was L. O. Fuselier, the legendary district attorney from Evangeline Parish and a long-time acquaintance of Laborde. During Laborde's presentation to the Commission, he was peppered by questions from Fuselier. Becoming exasperated, C. E. said, "L.O., you don't know nothing about tax assessments." Fuselier's instant reply: "Well, neither do you, C.E."

Cliff Laborde
Lafayette

Back in the 1940s, before the Caddo Parish courthouse was air conditioned, the courtroom windows were kept open to ventilate the heat in the summertime. One Monday morning, argument day, a colorful lawyer was arguing to the judge about the interpretation of an article of the Code of Practice. He argued that the words of the article should be applied literally, but his opponent argued that although the words said what they said, surely the legislature did not intend the words to be taken literally.

After hearing the arguments back and forth, the jurist finally told the lawyer: "I know that the article says what you say. But surely the legislature did not intend for such a result as you want. Therefore, your exception is denied."

The lawyer looked at the judge, loudly slammed the Code of Practice volume shut, and tossed it out the open window, saying: "Guess we won't be needin' that anymore."

Justice Jeffrey Victory
Shreveport

Philip Saal and I were trying a case involving reconduction of an agricultural lease. We represented the landowner, Noble Chambers from Crowley represented the farmer, and Judge Bradford "Bumpy" Ware was presiding.

At one point during the trial, Chambers stood up and told the court about a new case in the advance sheets which furthered his argument in the case. Philip immediately jumped up and objected. When asked the basis of his objection, Philip, with a straight face, looked at Judge Ware and stated that "its's no fair using advance sheets in a trial." The tension of the trial evaporated.

Ed Saal
Gueydan

Judge Jacques Weiner of Shreveport provided these four classic stories of argument in the U. S. Fifth Circuit.

Judge Grady Jolly (who originally hails from north Mississippi) was presiding over a panel of the Fifth Circuit which was hearing argument on a case in which the appellant was represented by a lawyer from North Mississippi Legal Services. The lawyer was widely known in those parts for questionable practices (sometimes implicating mendacity) and for pursuing cases close to (or crossing) the line separating vigorous advocacy from frivolous and unmeritorious litigation. In fact, he was before the Fifth Circuit on the day in question appealing a large attorneys' fee sanction for having prosecuted litigation "for the sole purpose of harassment." During the course of counsel's argument, Judge Jolly interrupted and read from the record a long list of counsel's improper conduct, including harassment, delay, missing of deadlines, falsehoods, and the like, then stated, "Counsel, it sounds like you were just flat lying!" Without hesitation, the lawyer responded, "Your Honor, I ain't never said that I stand before this court as no perfect man!"

Shortly before Alabama, Georgia, and Florida were split from the Fifth Circuit to form the Eleventh Circuit, the "old" Fifth was sitting en banc – 26 judges! – and rehearing a case in which the original panel had divided, Judge Wisdom having written for the majority and future Chief Judge Charles Clark having written for the dissent. Counsel for the party who had lost in the original panel hearing (the party championed by Judge Clark in his dissent) was at the lectern. Each time Judge Wisdom would interrupt and ask a piercing question, Judge Clark would follow by feeding counsel a "softball" question. After several such exchanges counsel was finally backed into a corner and Judge Wisdom asked a question, figuratively pinning counsel to the legal wall. In forlorn desperation, the lawyer looked at Judge Clark and asked, "What do <u>we</u> say to that?"

In a case being heard on oral argument by the Fifth Circuit in the 1980s, a rustic minority attorney of advanced age from rural Mississippi was expounding in a style more reminiscent of a country preacher than an appellate lawyer. Each time during the course of his argument that he referred to a prior Fifth Circuit opinion, he said, "And in the case of <u>Smith v. Jones</u>, Your Honors <u>alleged</u> " so and so, "and in the case of <u>Roe v. Doe</u>, Your Honors <u>alleged</u>" so and so. Finally, the late Judge Homer Thornberry, in his very soft and courteous manner, interrupted and admonished, "Counsel, this court does not 'allege'; parties allege; we <u>find</u> or <u>hold</u>."

At that, the lawyer took one large step back from the lectern, bowed deeply at the waist, touched his palms together in a prayerful pose, and said: "Beggin' Your Honor's opinion and pardon; this court alleges; the big court in Washington holds!" Judge Thornberry, in his ever kind manner, just smiled.

A three-judge panel of the Fifth Circuit, with Judge Tom Reavley presiding, entered the courtroom in New Orleans promptly at nine o'clock, was seated following the "Oyez," with counsel for appellant and appellee for the first case already seated at respective counsel tables. While Judge Reavley made the customary pre-argument remarks concerning the number of cases to be heard, the court's "lighting" system for keeping counsel apprised of time, and the like, counsel for appellant was shuffling papers and books preparatory to going to the lectern. When the preliminary remarks were completed, Judge Reavley announced, "We'll now hear the first case of the day, <u>Jones v. Smith</u>, and the court recognizes Mr. X for the appellant." Mr. X, however, was still busy arranging his papers to take them from counsel table to the lectern and did not look up. Judge Reavley repeated, "The court recognizes Mr. X, counsel for appellant," but Mr. X continued to fuss with his folders and papers without looking up. Judge Reavley then upped the volume and in his east Texas baritone firmly stated, "THE COURT RECOGNIZES MR. X!," upon which Mr. X looked up, broke into a broad smile, walked directly from counsel table to the bench, extended his right hand to Judge Reavley, and stated gratefully, "Mercy me, Your Honor, wherever from?" (Since that incident, most presiding judges at the Fifth Circuit have dropped "recognizes" and open with "The Court will hear from Mr. X, counsel for appellant.")

During the early 1980s, the U. S. Fifth Circuit followed a practice in en banc cases of not interrupting the first one-half of counsel's oral argument with questions. In one instance, counsel's presentation had nothing to do with the issue upon which the court had determined to hear the case before the full court. Two of the judges did not wish to appear totally disinterested in the argument. One penciled a note to the other, offering a challenge to see which of the two could first list all of Louisiana's 64 parishes, and their respective parish seats. With a nod the race began. A few minutes later, as appellant's counsel droned on, one of his co-counsel leaned over and whispered in another's ear: "I don't know about the other judges, but those two over there seem to be writing down just about everything our colleague is saying."

The lawyer who made the following remarks in a closing argument was Social Security eligible, prone to nip on the bottle and to do little legal research, but to bellow like a bull when he was before a jury. The trial was of a deputy sheriff on a corruption charge, which, of course, violated federal law.

Ladies and gentlemen, if He who made the moon and the sun and hung the stars on high could be merciful and just, then so can you. I submit to you ladies and gentlemen of the jury that if you convict [this defendant] on the testimony of thieves, rogues, whores and disgruntled politicians, that never again will the nightingale of a clear conscience perch upon your pillow to sing you to sleep at night, but that the ghosts of the wicked and the perjured shall be your companions until your dying eyes shall turn to read the rapt and mystic meaning of the stars.

6. A Most Unforgettable Character

John B. (Spike) Scofield of Lake Charles provides these vignettes about one of the unforgettable members of the Bar:

> Jack Rogers was one of the most distinct characters ever to practice law. He graduated from LSU Law School at or near the top of his class and was extremely smart, a fact that he hid better than anyone I've ever known. His country bumpkin demeanor was so pronounced that one quickly formed the impression that it had to be an act, a put on. It wasn't. He spoke in a high, nasal twang that would have been considered an exaggeration even on the TV show "Hee Haw."

> Jack was a sloppy dresser and often, especially when appearing in court, he would scratch his head with a pencil and then put that end of the pencil into his mouth. Not a pretty sight. When asked how he was doing, Jack would screech a reply, "I'm starvin' to death," or "The wolves are at the door," or "It's a hard life," or "I can't make a livin'." With all of this, Jack had a weird but keen sense of humor. In sum, I was crazy about him.

Rogers Story No. 1:

> Jack's practice consisted mainly of handling separations and divorces and most of those were uncontested. It was not unusual for Jack to handle 15 to 20 uncontested divorces in one day. He had a secretary

who was efficient in taking all of the necessary information from the clients at Jack's office and when it came time to appear in court, she would go with Jack, primarily for the purpose of pointing out the clients to him. Jack took considerable pride in speeding through these hearings without wasting a word. For the most part, his cryptic questioning was essentially the same for each client and became so routine that Jack paid little or no attention to the answers.

One day Jack was going through this ritual and it went something like this:

Jack:	What is your name?
Witness:	Sylvia Smith.
Jack:	Where do you live?
Witness:	1206 Center Street, Lake Charles, Louisiana.
Jack:	When were you married?
Witness:	August 2, 1975.
Jack:	Are you living with your husband now?
Witness:	No.
Jack:	Did he move out?
Witness:	Yes.
Jack:	When did he move out?
Witness:	November 3, 1979?
Jack:	Did you do anything to cause him to leave?
Witness:	No.
Jack:	Have you lived together since he left?
Witness:	No.

Jack:	Now, Mrs. Boudreaux, do you want this court to grant to you a legal separation?
Witness:	I'm not Mrs. Boudreaux.
Jack:	(His high pitched twang much higher and louder than usual) *You ain't Mrs. Boudreaux?*
Witness:	No.
Jack:	Who are you?
Witness:	I'm Sylvia Smith.
Jack:	(After Jack and his secretary frantically shuffled through the files piled in front of him, and eventually found the right file) You are Sylvia Smith and your husband is Thomas Smith?
Witness:	Yes.
Jack:	If I asked you as Mrs. Smith the same questions I asked you as Mrs. Boudreaux, would your answers be the same?
Witness:	Yes.
Court Reporter:	Your Honor, because of the laughter in the courtroom, I did not hear the last question and answer.

Rogers Story No. 2:

Occasionally Jack would handle a case other than a separation or divorce. Once he represented a Jones Act claimant in federal court before Judge Edwin F. Hunter, Jr. At a status conference with a number of other attorneys representing various defendants, the discussion turned to whether Jack's client, who worked offshore, would qualify as a seaman and, specifically, how Jack's client traveled to and from the offshore platform on which he was injured. Judge Hunter questioned each defense lawyer to determine if that lawyer's client had been responsible for transporting the plaintiff to the platform by boat. After each of the attorneys *denied* that their respective clients had anything to do with transporting plaintiff to the platform, Jack offered, "Well, Judge, I guess he was just borned out there."

7. The Day of the Cuspidor

Wade Mouton of Kaplan provides the story of "The Day of the Cuspidor:"

> In the mid to late '70s, I was seated in one of the attorneys' chairs in the courtroom, waiting my turn for morning hour in Judge Carroll Spell's court. There were about 15 or 20 lawyers waiting in line, and the packed courtroom came to a hush when His Honor took the Bench. Into the double doors from the hallway comes Roger Sellers, who was late and was trying to be inconspicuous. As he opened the swinging doors for entry into the bench and bar area, and in his attempt to move swiftly to an unoccupied seat to his left, Roger had the misfortune of kicking a cuspidor. I have no idea of what Roger's athletic abilities are, but on this fateful day, the cuspidor sailed through the air in a fashion similar to balls kicked by place kickers in the NFL, and hit the center of Judge Spell's bench. The cover of the cuspidor flew up in the air, and the contents of the cuspidor caused attorneys from that point on to make a big circle while approaching the bench. Judge Spell, without flinching, looked at Roger and asked, "DO YOU REST, MR. SELLERS?"
>
> On that fateful day, I happened to be seated next to Barrett Harrington. Barrett joined the multitudes in the

courtroom laughing, as Roger's ears turned red and he apologized to the court. The only problem was that when everyone else stopped laughing, Barrett could not contain himself and continued to laugh or snicker for about 15 minutes. I was cowering in my chair as Judge Spell kept casting an evil eye in our direction. However, as a green horn lawyer sitting next to an accomplished attorney, I could do nothing but pray that the judge would not think I was part of a conspiracy with Barrett.

Barrett's confirmation of default then came up, and he placed his briefcase on the plaintiff's table, approximately nine or 10 feet from the Judge's bench and approximately three feet from the area where the spoils of the cuspidor graced the floors of the courtroom. Barrett completed his case and as he slipped his documents back into his briefcase, Judge Spell asked him a question. Barrett turned around to respond, and in the distraction forgot to secure the latches on his briefcase. When he then turned around again to leave, he picked up the briefcase and swung to his right, thereby throwing every document in his briefcase onto the floor and into the spilled contents of the cuspidor. The courtroom once again went into an uproar and everyone, with the exception of Barrett, was laughing.

While I am sure that many who experienced the drama outlined above have simply written it off as being "The Day of the Cuspidor," I cannot help but feel that the humility experienced by these two gentlemen on that fateful day played a part in the outstanding careers that each has had, Barrett as City Court Judge in Crowley, and Roger as City Court Judge in Abbeville.

8   Some Colorful Comments

One of my favorite memories is based on positions in a case involving 18 vehicles and approximately 25 lawyers. One of the drivers being deposed was a young lady who was employed at the local racetrack. She testified that her job involved exercising the horses, and she was known as a "Pony Girl." During her deposition, one of our local lawyers who had a reputation for bearing down heavily on a deponent grilled the young lady extensively and forcefully. Not unexpectedly she broke down crying, and the deposition had to be interrupted to allow her an opportunity to regain her composure. At the conclusion of her deposition one of the lawyers in attendance, reflecting on the unnecessarily tough examination, opined: "I'll bet that is the first time that a Pony Girl has ever been cross-examined by a Horse's Ass!"

Earl Pitre
Lake Charles

Sometimes lawyers can forget where they are. Once during a heated debate before a United States district judge, at the Federal Courthouse, in the judge's conference room, with approximately ten other attorneys representing various parties, an attorney, frustrated by another lawyer's position on a stay pending appeal to the Fifth Circuit Court of Appeals, raised his voice and asked, "Why are you trying to make a federal case out of this?"

Jay Greenleaf of Shreveport tells this story about Ray Barlow, an articulate oil and gas attorney and the source of many quick retorts and memorable stories. On one occasion, however, Barlow did not have a ready comeback:

Ray was appointed to represent a taxi cab driver who was charged with transporting a prostitute across state lines in violation of the Mann Act. It was a bench trial in federal court in Shreveport before Judge Ben C. Dawkins, Jr. In the course of arguing the case, Ray was questioning the veracity of the alleged "lady of the evening," and he said to Judge Dawkins, "Your Honor, this is the worst prostitute I've ever known!" Without missing a beat, Judge Dawkins asked Ray, "Well, Mr. Barlow, just exactly how many prostitutes have you known in your life?" Uncharacteristically, Ray was speechless.

9. Potpourri

Here are some stories too good to leave out.

A suit against Crown-Zellerbach arose when a large bundle of paper bags, weighing approximately 500 pounds, tipped over and fell and injured a warehouse man. A defense lawyer, becoming very frustrated with a witness' evasive answers, declared: "If this case does not have anything to do with the laws of gravity, I am a monkey's uncle." Instantly, one of the plaintiff lawyers said: "Judge, we will stipulate to that."

Judge Louis Doherty
Baton Rouge

C. E. Laborde's Marksville office frequently was used by out of town lawyers for depositions. On one occasion C. E. returned from lunch and found two of such lawyers and a court reporter sitting in his library, awaiting the deponent. When asked who they were deposing, one attorney told C. E. the name of a then well-known Louisiana politician. C . E.'s immediate response was: "Don't waste your time swearing him in."

Cliffe Laborde
Lafayette

Beth, my wife and partner, was representing a man who, on the spur of the moment or, more than likely in a rather inebriated state, married a woman who he had just met at a local bar. As it turned out, she was more of a bar fly than a wife and her extracurricular activity was the driving force in the divorce action. She was represented by another local attorney. On the date of the trial, Beth was telling some of the funny stories about the case to other attorneys waiting for their cases to be heard. About that time, the defendant's attorney walked up. One of the young attorneys began teasing the defendant's attorney about his client and her extracurricular activities. About that time, a woman walked in wearing a very short leather skirt, black mesh stockings, and a very revealing low cut blouse. This young attorney turned to the defense attorney representing the defendant in my wife's case, lowered his voice and, indicating the woman who had just walked in, asked, "Is that your client?" The defendant's attorney replied, "Oh, no, that's my wife." The startled reaction of the lawyer audience should have been captured on video for later use; it was a story in itself.

Bob Thomas
Lake Charles

The wife of a newly-admitted lawyer went to court to watch her husband in action on one of his very first trial court appearances. She was overcome by the solemnity of the occasion, with all of its judicial trappings. As she walked down the center aisle of the court room to take her seat to watch the "excitement" of rule day, she apparently forgot momentarily where she was because, upon arriving at the chosen row, she genuflected before taking her seat.

Pat Ottinger
Lafayette

A panel of the U.S. Fifth Circuit on which Judge Reavley was presiding was scheduled to hear an appeal from the Eastern District of Texas in which the personal injury plaintiff was represented by a country lawyer well known to Judge Reavley, also an east Texan. The lawyer was more proficient at "boozing" than advocacy, and the instant argument was no exception. This particular morning he showed up <u>sans</u> coat or tie, but the Clerk of

Court provided him with both. When his turn came, the lawyer proceeded to make a terrible and feckless argument, and the court's opinion "pouring him out" likely arrived in his office before he did. As fate would have it, Judge Reavley encountered this tippling East Texan at a professional function shortly thereafter and, as a matter of small talk, assured the lawyer that his attire had not been the cause of the court's adverse judgment. In an overly-candid response, the lawyer replied, "Well, that would have been a better reason than the one y'all gave in your opinion!"

Judge Jacques Weiner
Shreveport

Louisiana lawyers frequently hold meetings on foreign soil, with London, Paris, Venice and Rome as the most popular spots. During one such visit to London, the Louisiana law group planned a closing dinner at a famous palace a considerable distance into the countryside. To make the trip from the meeting hotel to the palace, the group chartered several cars of the Orient Express. The time of departure from a London train station was 6 p.m. The Louisiana group was dressed in formal wear, and their cars were stocked with champagne and other party amenities. As luck would have it, a commuter train loaded with blue collar workers heading home for the weekend was loading on the track next to the Orient Express. Standing person to person and holding on to overhead straps, the London working persons gazed somewhat enviously (or at least curiously) at the goings on in the Orient Express. One Louisiana lawyer, noticing their interest, lifted his glass to them in a mock toast of salutation. Instantly, at least two dozen middle fingers extended upward from the working class car, in the direction of the Orient Express. Undaunted, the Louisiana lawyer expressed his reaction: "Poverty sucks."

10. Claims and Defenses

Bob Dunkelman of Shreveport describes the deposition he took of a plaintiff who had changed lawyers several times and was then unrepresented. The plaintiff testified that he had last taken his file to another attorney (a retired state district court judge) who had reviewed the file for him and, after looking at the file, advised plaintiff that his case "was like an alligator without arms or legs." I asked the plaintiff what he understood that phrase to mean. He responded that the attorney (retired judge) had explained to him that it meant that "his case was difficult to wrestle with, but that it wouldn't be going anywhere."

Judge Peter Beer reminds us of the "woodwork defense":

> I discovered the defense when I was involved in a jury trial before Judge Herbert Christenberry. There were a number of plaintiffs and a number of defendants and, thus, a large number of lawyers were involved. My hope was to keep a very low profile so that my defendant client would not appear to have any responsibility for the ghastly accident. Each day of trial my courtroom posture further lessened so that by week's end, as the case made its way to the jury, I was almost out of sight; I had asked no questions and made no objections, and I was feeling pretty good about my strategy.
>
> When A. R. Christovich, Sr. rose to speak to the jury, he pointed his finger at me and said: "You see that lawyer who has almost disappeared into the woodwork. Why, he is as tall as any average lawyer even though you'd think he's only about 3 feet tall. That's because he is embarked on what is called the woodwork defense. He just hopes that he'll fade into the woodwork and you'll forget all about his negligent client who is the real culprit in this case."
>
> It got me right between the eyes. It was my last effort to get away with a "woodwork" defense.

Spoliation (destruction of evidence, intentional or accidental) has become an important concept in the law. One of the earliest and most unusual cases of possible spoliation may have been when, during prohibition, a colorful defense attorney's client was charged with making the forbidden booze. Just prior to a recess, the prosecutor offered into evidence a bottle containing several ounces of liquid and then rested the government's case. It was a hot day (no air conditioning then), and everyone except the defense counsel left the courtroom for a cold drink in a cooler place. Upon resumption of the trial, defense counsel confirmed that the state had rested and then moved for an acquittal for lack of any evidence that a prohibited product had been manufactured. The prosecutor, obviously puzzled, waved his arm towards the bottle he had offered into evidence just before the recess. Defense counsel's response was very simple: "Empty bottles are proof of nothing." Indeed the bottle was empty. The client was acquitted for lack of essential evidence.

Harry V. Booth and Samuel P. Love, Sr. (known affectionately as "Mr. Harry" and "Mr. Sam," respectively) were two of the most seasoned trial lawyers in north Louisiana during the 1960's. Mr. Harry had a broad, diversified trial practice; Mr. Sam largely focused on domestic and criminal cases. They were trying a particularly hotly contested domestic case before one of the kindest, most patient district judges ever to sit in Caddo Parish, Judge Robert J. O'Neal. The case went on for several days with fierce debate on the cause of action, largely fueled by disputes over the property in an obviously large community of acquets and gains. Their files were voluminous and covered the counsel table at which both sat. The files "spilled over." Judge O'Neal had cautioned counsel on several occasions about the intensity of their arguments, on even minor legal points. Finally "it hit the fan." Mr. Sam was looking for a document to use in cross-examination and he mistakenly (?) reached over into one of Mr. Harry's files. Mr. Harry saw this and said, "Sam, get your blasted hands out of my files!" Mr. Sam quickly withdrew his hand and said, "There's nothing in your files 'cause you don't have a case and you know it." Judge O'Neal's patience expired. In a quiet voice he said: "That's enough gentlemen. I find you both in contempt and fine you $10 or one hour in jail." Mr. Sam pulled out his wallet and handed the clerk a $10 bill. Mr . Harry continued with his questioning of the witness. As the trial day drew to a close, the evidence was concluded and Judge O'Neal took the case under advisement. As they gathered up their files, Mr. Sam said to Judge O'Neal, "Are you gonna make Harry pay or does he go to jail?" Judge O'Neal hesitated as he was descending the bench and asked, "Have you paid, Mr. Booth?" Mr. Harry said he thought he had. Judge O'Neal inquired of the clerk, who quietly answered "Not yet, Judge." At that point Mr. Harry handed the clerk the required coinage. They all then walked out of the courtroom, counsel bade their clients farewell, and the two counsel walked out of the courthouse together. Mr. Harry said: "Why did you do that Sam? I was going to buy us each a drink with that $10." To which Mr. Sam immediately responded: "Damn, Harry, why didn't you say something. If I had known that, I wouldn't have told the Judge!"

As Dean Hebert once remarked, the legal profession "is not known for its sobriety." Partaking of the grape has brought the end to many a legal career, but others have endured and prevailed. Thus it was said of a certain lawyer: "Sober, he's the best lawyer in Louisiana. Drunk, he's the second best lawyer in Louisiana."

CHAPTER VI
THE JUDGES

1. The Changing Face of the Judiciary

One of the most significant changes in the Louisiana judicial system, in the 40+ years since the assemblers of this collection of law lore entered the legal profession, has been the change in the face of the judiciary. The change has been from white, middle-aged male judiciary to a broad mixture of the old with the new – black, young and female. The changing faces have not changed the relationship between lawyers and the judges, who are the most dominant figures in the system. Perhaps this is best illustrated by a story told by Judge Robin Giarusso of New Orleans.

> When I was first elected to the bench, there were few women judges. Often, when I was out socially, a lawyer would kiss me hello and comment that they had never kissed a judge before...that is until my dear friend the late Dermot McGlinchey noted in his wonderful Irish brogue, "My son, we've been kissing judges forever, but in a different part of their anatomy."

Judge Giarusso shares another humorous encounter:

> In our Court, junior judges are assigned to the domestic relations docket. As a domestic relations judge, I came to know the litigants fairly well due to the nature of the proceedings. Unlike other civil matters, the litigants appear in court often. They come for the initial settings of child support, alimony and use of the home. In those days, they came once for the separation and again for the divorce. They come for the custody hearing. And as the children grow up, as the parents change jobs, lose jobs, remarry or relocate, they come for rules to lower or raise the alimony and child support, change custody, modify visitation, etc.

With this background in mind, one day I was walking down the corridor of the Courthouse. One of those frequent litigants was sitting on the benches. She looked up, told me good morning and then said, "Judge, you sure look different with your clothes on." Of course, I turned scarlet and somehow managed to say, "You mean I look different without my robe."

Judge Bill Brown of Baton Rouge tells a similar story:

Several years ago I spoke to the Daughters of the American Revolution. After my presentation several people came forward to meet me and/or comment about my remarks. One lady introduced herself as having served on a jury I had presided over, and commented to me, "I did not recognize you with your clothes on." After overcoming her embarrassment, she said... "without your robe."

Judge Coleman Lindsey served on the 19th Judicial District Court (Baton Rouge) for many years. In appearance, he was small, thin, wrinkled, and looked like someone's yard man dressed in judicial robes. In fact, gardening was his favorite past time. He kept an immaculate yard at his home on Stanford Avenue, the main street that leads to "College Town" near LSU. On weekends, and quite often on afternoons, he could be seen in the most disreputable clothes, puttering in his yard, keeping everything meticulously clean and flowers blooming.

He loved to tell the story of a lady who one day stopped her car and called him to the car window. She said that she had been noticing the beautiful work that he had been doing in the yard, and that she wanted to know what "the lady of the house" paid him? His immediate response, in his best judicial voice, which was impressive, was, "Here, the lady of the house gives me BEDROOM privileges." He took delight for years in thinking that maybe he had caused a bit of scandalous gossip.

Judge Lindsey had a very strong opinion of psychiatrists and the whole psychiatric field–a fact I learned the hard way. After the case in which I made that discovery, he confessed in chambers that he simply did not believe in psychiatrists. He said that their definition of sanity would have him in the "nut house" in no time at all.

In that case, I had a client who fell three stories while on a construction job, and landed on his back on a pile of building materials. The x-rays revealed there were no broken bones or obvious injuries. After about six weeks of recovery, the doctors said he could return to work, but he insisted he could not. He came to my office to complain of his resulting loss of compensation. Then with great emotion, he informed me that he not only could not work, but that he had completely lost his ability to perform the sexual act! He was from West Baton Rouge Parish and looked like a linebacker, weighing at least 230 pounds and standing about 6 feet tall. It was a moving interview.

I immediately sent him to a psychiatrist to invoke the newly discovered "traumatic neurosis" basis for Workmen's Compensation. Our psychiatrist made such a diagnosis, and during trial, he put tremendous emphasis on the fact the man claimed he was impotent. He stated that since such a symptom was not readily admitted by men in my client's educational and social strata, he believed the complaints were genuine.

After Judge Lindsey quickly dispatched the case, we went to the First Circuit Court of Appeals. My opposing counsel was Pat Wilson, one of the senior partners of Breazeale, Sachse, and Wilson. After I finished my opening argument, which included what I modestly viewed as a brilliant discourse on the importance of impotence, Pat, with court approval, put up a motion picture screen, and with a small film projector began to present pictures of my client taken during the sugar cane harvesting season. There was my client in all his glory, swinging huge weights around like babies and otherwise performing feats of strength, all of which were most devastating to the basic contention of his inability to work.

After the completion of the film, Judge Paul B. Landry, one of the three sitting judges, leaned across the bench and with a twinkle in his eye, asked, "Mr. Wilson, do you have any films to rebut Mr. Benton's erection theory?"

Thomas H. Benton
Baton Rouge

John Dixon, who served on the Second Circuit Court of Appeals and later became a Justice and Chief Justice of the Supreme Court, began his judicial career on the district bench in Caddo parish. On one Wednesday afternoon, he was handling a large number of uncontested cases, many of which were separation/alimony/child support actions. A significant number of the cases were based on the then abandonment article of the Civil Code. Judge Dixon always demanded that there be adequate proof of the abandonment, and not just a mutual separation of the parties. He invariably did this by several carefully worded and direct questions after counsel concluded questioning. Needless to say, in more than a few cases the answers were such that Judge Dixon denied the separation judgment. The tension among the lawyers at that point in the proceedings was universal and real. Jesse Stone, then a young attorney, had his uncontested abandonment suit called. He put his client on the stand and carefully asked all relevant and critical questions. When he finished he kept his head down, as if looking at his notes, and said in a quiet, respectful voice, "I tender the witness." There was a noticeable gasp and all of the attorneys looked up at the bench with the proverbial "bated breath." They knew the sky was about to fall in. They were wrong. Judge Dixon smiled and said "No questions, judgment granted." The attorneys could not resist applauding.

2. The Federal Judges

The esteem in which some federal judges are held is illustrated by this story from Judge Louis Doherty (retired) of Baton Rouge:

A number of years ago I was conducting a pre-trial conference involving mostly New Orleans lawyers. I mentioned that the F.B.I. had questioned me about the nomination of a lawyer for the Eastern District and I had given him a very favorable recommendation. One of the lawyers declared: "_____ is such a nice fellow, it will take him at least six months to become a S.O.B."

I understand that he is still a nice fellow and that the job has not gone to his head.

Judge Peter Beer of New Orleans recalls the dynamics of Judge Herbert Christenberry of the federal district court in New Orleans:

If you tried a case before Judge Christenberry you soon became aware of his special treatment of witnesses he did not believe. He would wait until the witness made a particularly outlandish observation, and then would spin his chair around so as to give the witness his back. This pretty much let the jury know what the judge thought about that testimony. Thereafter, the judge could, at his pleasure, deliver the coup de gras by waiting for another thoroughly outlandish observation in the course of which he would slowly turn from his original position of giving the witness his back and stare incredulously at the hapless individual without saying a word. I don't recall that any lawyer ever had the nerve to put this on the record. I doubt that anyone ever did. Furthermore, I'd guess that the judge was right about 100% of the time.

Judge Christenberry seemed to identify with the jury early in the case and gave the impression (correctly) that he was there to be sure that the jury wasn't hornswoggled. And he could put you back 10 squares with one brief observation. Example: "Counsel, saying it out loud and saying it often doesn't make it so."

Another Judge Christenberry story involves another unforgettable judge, Coleman Lindsey of the Nineteenth Judicial District Court. Both judges were dedicated to processing cases and keeping their dockets clear. Judge Lindsey achieved his goal by refusing to allow lawyers to set a case for trial in his division until they had first "pre-tried" the case with him (one must remember that this was long before the pre-trial conference became a standard procedure). One day a lawyer appeared in Judge Lindsey's court and moved to assign a case for trial. When the judge reminded him of his rule, and asked that he see the judge after court, the lawyer stuck by his guns, insisting that under the law he had the right to assign a case for trial during "morning (motion and rule) hour." Judge Lindsey backed down somewhat, telling the lawyer, "You can go ahead and assign it but I can guarantee we'll try the case on that date, and no excuses." Fast forward several months. The date selected by the lawyer was approaching, but the lawyer was in the midst of a trial in Judge Christenberry's court. The federal trial should have ended the day before the state court trial date, but it did not. The lawyer was "on the horns of a dilemma." The unwritten rule was that a continuing case in one jurisdiction would "bump" the assignment for trial in the other. Thus when the lawyer asked Judge Christenberry to continue the case, he was rejected, based upon the rule. Yet the lawyer was certain that given Judge Lindsey's temperament and the "slight" which he had given the judge, there would be no continuance of the state court case. The following morning the lawyer appeared in state court and sent one of his employees to federal court to announce – to a packed courtroom – that the lawyer would not be in Judge Christenberry's court that day because he had to try a case in state court. Judge Christenberry, of course, administered the most severe punishment available. Rumor has it that he would have disbarred the lawyer from federal court if leaders of the Baton Rouge bar had not intervened.

Another of Judge Peter Beer's reminisces about a prominent federal judge:

> When Judge Skelly Wright began to hold pretrial conferences as one of the two judges at the U.S. District Court, he generated an interest on the part of Alvin Rubin, who later became a U.S. District Judge, and then a member of the Fifth Circuit Court of Appeals. Alvin really elevated the status of the pretrial conference as an instrument for settlement of cases; he just about insisted that cases – especially personal injury cases – be settled.

One day after a sort of rocky pretrial conference, he ordered Fred Gesivius, John Hainkel and me to settle a case without any further wasting of valuable time. We tried hard to do so and finally, painfully, frustratingly, it got done. Thereupon, we sent Rubin a very large illustrated cartoon showing all three of us being treated for severe bodily injuries at Charity Hospital Emergency room and asking one of the nurses if she would please call Judge Rubin's office to let him know that we had come to an amicable settlement per his instructions.

He loved the cartoon, had it framed, and kept it on his office wall for a long time. I'm not exactly sure but I still think it was a left-handed compliment when he bragged about getting a settlement from the likes of Gisevius, Hainkel and Beer.

Federal courts have jurisdiction over duck hunting violations, the penalty for which can be stiff. In addition, some federal judges are avid duck hunters. Here are a couple of stories arising out of that combination:

As a young lawyer in Lafayette in about 1968, I was purchasing my shotgun shells for the upcoming duck season. As I stood at the "check out" line with case of 12 gauge shotgun shells, I noted that Federal Judge Richard Putnam was immediately behind me. At that time I had probably appeared before him two or three times. He was the only federal judge in the Lafayette District at that time.

I had prior knowledge that Judge Putnam was an avid duck hunter and enjoyed hunting in the southwest Louisiana marshes below Abbeville every year. I noticed he was purchasing one box of shotgun shells and that they were "duck loads." I respectfully addressed Judge Putnam and began inquiring as to where he was going to be hunting ducks the opening weekend of the season. He really didn't directly reply to my inquiry, but simply made note that I was purchasing an entire case of shotgun shells for the upcoming season. He then commented that it was his understanding the limit was four ducks per day, and he normally only took 5 shells with him to the blind, the extra or fifth shell being for a possible "cripple." He further noted that I was obviously planning to do a lot of shooting and perhaps my aim was not that good.

Taking his comments as an apparent warning not to deplete the population of ducks in south Louisiana to the extent of shooting more than the daily bag limit, I replied, in somewhat of a stutter, that my shells weren't entirely for me, that I planned to use them for the entire season, and that I probably wasn't that good of a shot. I smiled and quickly left the store.

Richard Chappius
Lafayette

If you're not a duck hunter, you probably cannot understand the passion with which the sport is embraced by its devotees. One story illustrates this. While practicing law in the Cajun Country, an attorney was contacted by a "big city" lawyer whose "big city" client had a country problem: the client had been caught at his hunting camp with an over-the-limit bag. (The story was that the culprit was the client's customer, but the client accepted the blame.) At any rate, the "going rate" for that violation, before a federal judge, was 30 days in jail. The "big city" lawyer explained to the rural attorney that his client was the head of a multi-million dollar business corporation and could not afford to go to jail. In essence, he would do anything to stay out of jail. The rural attorney approached the judge with an equally enthusiastic plea for the new client, and the judge met him halfway; he would not send the client to jail, but the client would have to pay a hefty fine and forfeit duck hunting privileges for the following season. The client was delighted and the checks were promptly received. Fast forward six months. The rural attorney receives a call from the "big city" lawyer reminding him of the joint client, and putting this request: "Our client can't bear to miss hunting this season. He has put all of his business in order, and is ready to go to jail for 30 days if he can hunt the coming season." Somewhat timidly, the local attorney called the judge and explained the request. Instead of ire, which was expected, he heard a roaring laugh, with the judge's comment: "Tell him he can hunt!"

Judge Edwin F. Hunter, Jr. was appointed by President Eisenhower and served on the bench longer than nearly any other federal judge. Before Judge Hunter took senior status, he would regularly have motion days on which he would hear oral arguments on as many as 15 to 20 motions. These motion days became legendary in the Western District of Louisiana. Judge Hunter would have read every brief and was razor sharp on all of the issues in each and every case, no matter how intricate. Lawyers were known to attend these motion days even though they did not have a motion to argue.

A local lawyer (we'll call him Sam Adams) was famous for being late for everything – trials, motions, depositions, appointments, etc. He also began to bald at a relatively early age. He eventually decided to buy a toupeé and his first public appearance after the purchase was one of Judge Hunter's motion days. Sam, as usual, arrived late, after arguments in other motions were well underway.

Resplendent in his new wig, Sam came through the double doors in the rear of the courtroom while Judge Hunter and at least 30 lawyers were listening to an impassioned argument being made by a lawyer in support of a motion. While the lawyer orated on, Judge Hunter looked up to see Sam coming through the door and the judge shouted, drowning out the presentation of the lawyer at the rostrum, " Mr. Adams! Mr. Adams! What is that thing on your head?"

Sam was able to survive the uproarious laughter that ensued in the courtroom, but after that day, no one ever saw the toupeé again.

Some cases require little explanation or efforts at humanizing or adding bits and pieces of what we might call humor. Nothing need be added to or said about the following from an opinion by a Fifth Circuit panel composed of John R. Brown (author of the opinion), Irving H. Goldberg and the co-author of this collection of stories, in the case of <u>Black v. White</u>, No. 83-2412, an appeal from the Northern District of Texas.

The trial court's decision was as follows:

I. Findings of Fact
   a.. There was a contract.
   b. Under the contract, White had to pay money to Black.
   c. He did.
   d. White and Black are from different states.
II. Conclusions of Law
   a. White wins.

(signed)
District Judge

The appellant's brief contends:

As grounds of error, appellant would allege the following:

a..   The district court was wrong for three reasons.

   1. No substantial evidence to support the judgment.

   2. Jury's findings are clearly erroneous.

   3. The judge abused his discretion.

(signed)
Attorney for Appellant

The appellee's brief responds:

In response to appellant's allegations of error, appellee would submit the following:

a. No it wasn't.

   1. Yes, there was.

   2. No, they weren't.

   3. No, he didn't.

(signed)
Attorney for Appellee

Appellant's reply brief insists:

To what we said in our initial brief:

Ditto. Moreover, we add that

a) it was;

1) there wasn't;

2) there were;

3) he did. So there.

(signed)
Attorney for Appellant

The decision of the Court of Appeals, in its entirety opined:

I. FACTS

The facts of this case need not be repeated.

II. DISCUSSION

Appellant says that the judgment is not supported by substantial evidence. It was.

She says the jury's findings were clearly erroneous. They weren't.

She says the judge abused his discretion. He didn't.[3]

---

[3] See Green v. Maddox, 578 F.2d 495 (2d Cir. 1968) ("He didn't."); Teal v. Fallows, 524 F.2d 25 (9th Cir. 1963) (She didn't either); contra, Arnold v. Dickens, 625 F.Supp. 893 (N.D.N.D. 1973) ("'Tis."), rev'd 622 F.2d 789 (10th Cir. 1974) ("Tain't); Bunton v. Madison, 615 F.2d 83 (7th Cir. 1973) (Maybe, but we're

AFFIRMED.

Judge Goldberg was persuaded to specially concur, using five times as many words as the opinion.

This case, of course, falls within the gray area, a color antithetical and abhorrent to my beloved ex-chief. I am astounded at the color blindness of the hirsute descendant of Charles Evan Hughes. My colleague John suffers from the same malady as I do, and that is we have a great difficulty in executing the doctrine of succinctness in opinion writing. The opinion will shock a great many of his colleagues, but would disappoint me, expectant as I am that from his pen the rainbow would not a single hue miss. I care not one whit how this case is decided, save only that it not be color blind and colored bland, as in its present form.

I trust that this opinion will be my beloved brother Brown's last exercise in brevity, and that he will soon return to the grand old style of an extra word, an extra phrase and a colorful sprinkling of wit and humor that pervaded his opinions in ancient times. I take it that this is a single-shot departure from the Brown as we all know him and as we love him. No more single sentence opinions, Brown. Take another martini (Vera's and the doctor's permission assumed, of course) and let the Brownisms flow unimpeded.

3. Louisiana Supreme Court Justices

We have collected surprisingly few stories about state supreme court justices. Some of those stories are chronicled elsewhere (see Chapter IV). Here are a few stories about some of the "giants" of the

---

not sure."). The Supreme Court has declined to hear the issue.

Louisiana judiciary.

Chief Justice Charles O'Neill wrote an opinion in a case involving adultery in which the male had denied under oath that he had an affair with a married lady. The husband's lawyer attacked this testimony as being untruthful. Judge O'Neill, a gentleman of the old school, made this memorable comment, "Any man who would not lie under such circumstances is unworthy of belief."

Judge James E. Clark
Shreveport

Al Tate served on the Louisiana court of appeals, the Louisiana Supreme Court and on the U. S. Fifth Circuit until his untimely death in 1986. He was beloved as a person and idolized as a legal scholar. Unfortunately, Al's speaking style left something to be desired, probably because his mouth could not move as fast as his mind. After one meeting in which he lectured to a large group of Louisiana judges, he asked: "Any questions?" There was only one reply; a judge near the rear of the room asked, "Justice Tate, how is it you can write so clear and talk so cloudy?"

The following story gives some insight into Al the man:

When I was moving to Baton Rouge to begin teaching at the Law Center, George Pugh allowed Suzy (my wife), myself, and our children to stay at his home while George and Jean were in Europe. Later on, during the Fall Semester, the Law Center held a reception for former Louisiana Supreme Court Justice Fournet. Justice Al Tate was standing next to Justice Fournet introducing folks to him. When Suzy and I came to them, Al, with a twinkle in his eye, said to Fournet: "This is Chris and Suzy Blakesley – this past Summer, Chris slept in the same bed as my wife." We all laughed – all of us except for Suzy. Turns out that the Tates had stayed in the Pugh's home the week before we did and used the same bed.

Christopher L. Blakesley
J.Y. Sanders Professor of Law
LSU Law Center

4. The Courts of Appeal

Louisiana courts of appeal operate in isolation. Courtroom sessions are infrequent and clerk's offices are rarely visited, and many of the judges work from offices in their home towns. The lack of "traffic" with the practicing bar is illustrated by a telephone call an attorney received from a long time district judge who had recently been elected to the court of appeals. The judge asked the attorney if he would be kind enough to call him once a week. Asking why, the attorney received this response from the judge: "a fella can be dead a week up here and no one would know."

The loneliness got to Peter Beer when he served on the Fourth Circuit. As he tells the story:

> I went from the City Council to the State Court of Appeal and then to U.S. District Court and thoroughly enjoyed each assignment, though I must say that working on an appellate court is a little bit lonely. I was lucky to have Ed Stoulig, John Boutall and Jimmy Gulotta around when I was at the Fourth Circuit. Nobody could ask for better shipmates and when Preston Huft would come up to pinch-hit, we had an especially joyful time. They were fine judges and great friends. One day Jimmy and Ed and I comprised the panel that was to consider an appeal from a district court ruling that some pornographic films were a nuisance and thus should be restricted. All three of us took our work seriously, but I made the mistake of bringing a large supply of popcorn to the showing in Jimmy's chambers. He hit the ceiling – threw me and my popcorn out. It took weeks for me to get him and Ed Stoulig to even speak to me about it."

Contempt is rare in the appellate court, but Judge Preston Aucoin relates this story of his advocacy days:

Many years ago when I was a practicing attorney, I had six cases to argue before the Third Circuit one day. I think I had the whole docket for that day. When I arrived I learned that Judge Guy Humphries (not particularly known for his gentle treatment of attorneys) was sitting ad hoc. The clerk called the first case, and as I arrived at the rostrum, Judge Humphries immediately seized upon a passage of my brief which was, to say the least, not very complimentary to the trial judge (Judge Octave "Guffy" Pavy of Opelousas). I had stated in my brief that in his zeal to rule against my client the judge had done such and such.

Well, the wind went out of my sails when Judge Humphries threatened me with contempt, particularly since I had five other cases to argue before him and the two other judges that day. I approached the bench and told the panel that if there would be a contempt hearing against me, I wanted time to hire a lawyer, and receive due notice, etc. Judge Hood, the Chief Judge, was on the panel, and he agreed.

Anyway, I had to struggle through my five remaining cases with the constant reminder that I was in big time trouble. As soon as I finished my cases, I found a pay phone (we did not have cellular phones then) and called Guffy (Judge Pavy) and told him there was a pretty good chance I would be held in contempt for writing something about him in my brief.

Before giving me a chance to tell him what I had written, Guffy, in his hoarse, gruff voice, said, "Preston, did you call me a ... (using a slang word for a person who commits a crime against nature)? I answered "no", and he responded: "Well, don't' worry about anything."

Two or three days later I received a copy of a letter Judge Pavy had written to Judge Hood praising my practice before him and asking the Court of Appeal not to consider the contempt proceeding. After another two or three days, I received a letter from Judge Hood basically stating that upon Judge Pavy's recommendation, there would be no contempt proceeding against me.

Joel Gooch of Lafayette provides this memory of a colorful state court judge:

> Early in my career I had occasion to appear at the Third Circuit Court of Appeal. The case ahead of mine involved an appeal by a plaintiff represented by Richard Bertrand, who had been a State Representative and was the older brother of then Mayor Rayburn Bertrand of Lafayette. One of the three panelists of the Third Circuit was Judge Jerome Domengeaux. Judge Domengeaux had a very sizeable girth at that time. Richard Bertrand's plaintiff was a woman who had squeezed between a table and a wall to reach a chair that collapsed when she sat in it. While Bertrand was arguing his appeal, Judge Domengeaux interrupted him and said, "Richard, what was the distance between the table and the wall when your client maneuvered between the two to reach the chair?"

> Bertrand paused for a moment then responded, "Let me put it this way, Judge, you would have never made it to the chair."

> Judge Domengeaux loved humor, and he began to cackle, as did the entire courtroom.

> The incident made a particular impression upon me because I had not then practiced law long enough to realize that judges had a sense of humor and were receptive to being involved with humor.

Humor during oral argument in the Supreme Court is rare, but not unheard of. In one instance (perhaps is was because the Court was in special session at the LSU Law Center), a lawyer "brought the house down" with an unorthodox argument. The case was *Entrevia v. Hood*, remembered as a "strict liability for buildings" case involving a trespasser from Washington Parish and his date who, without permission, visited a semi-abandoned building in Tangipahoa Parish. Arguing for the defendant was Joe Simpson of Amite; he tells the rest of the story:

> When Justice Dennis asked me a highly technical question (you'll understand this after you read the case) about the duty of a landowner to a trespasser, I simply answered "what this case teaches me is that people from Washington Parish should not come over and use our vacant houses for illicit sexual purposes without paying rent!" This brought the house down, including all of the justices' wives, who were sitting only a few feet away.

One of the most colorful of all Louisiana judges was Judge J. Cleveland Frugé, long of the Third Circuit. Warren Perrin of Lafayette shares these memories of the judge:

> In 1972, with the kind help of Professor George Pugh, I was able to obtain a clerkship with Judge Frugé, the "Parrain" and uncle of Justice Albert Tate. In preparing for my clerkship, I inquired about Judge Frugé and was told that he was not known as a "high intellectual" judge, but was one of the most pragmatic and compassionate of our state's judges. Shortly after beginning my work, I was assigned to do research on a case involving a sole-proprietorship and a corporation. Diligently, I researched the two entities and explored all ramifications and contrasts of the two types of business enterprises. During my enthusiastic presentation of the law to Judge Frugé, I was interrupted with a question: "What is the *real* difference between a sole proprietorship and a corporation?" Before I could give him my response, he stated: "A proprietorship is a person with a soul who has to answer to a higher authority, while a corporation has no soul and exists *only* for the bottom line."

> One day in researching the issue of quantum on a case where a prostitute had been burned during an accident while she was "working," I told Judge Frugé that

the defense had made an excellent argument that the plaintiff should not be awarded damages because she was injured while engaged in a nefarious and illegal act. Judge Frugé's reply: "When burned, a prostitute hurts just as much as anyone else." The plaintiff's award of damages was affirmed.

A well-known federal appellate judge and jokester (and one of the authors of this work) once presided over a Fifth Circuit panel hearing arguments. As one lawyer waxed eloquently before the panel, the smoke detection system in the courtroom malfunctioned, causing the alarm system to ring loudly in the courtroom. As the lawyer stood perplexed, the federal judge told him: "Counsel, you have triggered our B.S. detector." Several weeks later, the same judge, speaking to a group of attorneys in the ground level meeting room of a hotel in a major city, related that story in his introductory remarks. Shortly after the laughter subsided and the judge had launched into his presentation, a fire truck roared past, its siren blaring and drowning out the judge's remarks. As soon as the noise subsided, the master of ceremonies turned to the judge and said, "Your Honor, that's our B.S. detector."

5. The Trial Judges

Most of the legal wit comes from the "trenches," i.e., the trial court in which lawyers, judge, clients and witnesses meet. Here is a sampling of the kinds of humorous events that occur each day in the "trenches:"

Judge Henry Roberts had a particularly droll sense of humor, and he loved to poke fun without cracking a smile. Friday was Rule Day in Orleans Civil District Court and lawyers sat in great numbers in each division, awaiting their turn to argue. On this particular morning, two senior members of the Bar were strenuously arguing a point of Succession law. Judge Roberts was clearly tiring of the effort, but the energy of the elderly combatants seemed to increase with every exchange. Finally, one of the lawyers turned to Judge Roberts in some frustration and admitted that he could not recall the exact reference to the article or statute upon which his much-belabored legal theory depended, but he told Judge Roberts that he would "stake his life" on the accuracy of his representation of the law.

Before his opponent could speak, Judge Roberts leaned across the bench toward his court reporter and observed: "Let the record reflect that if counsel is wrong, he forfeits his life."

It took most of five minutes before order was restored in the courtroom.

Paul Andersson
New Orleans

An insurance case was being tried before Judge Revius Ortigue of the Orleans CDC. Defense counsel was questioning one of his own witnesses when Judge Ortigue leaned over the bench and asked plaintiff's counsel, "Are you going to allow counsel to continue in this leading line of questioning?" The plaintiff's counsel stood up, and, with an indignant air, said, "No, your honor, I am not. I object to this leading line of questioning." Judge Ortigue replied, "Objection denied, because I had to tip you off!"

Murphy Burke
Baton Rouge

Judge Peter Beer shares this story:

Bunky Healy filed a most unusual pleading at the Civil District Court for the Parish of Orleans. It was entitled "An Extraordinary Writ" and resulted from a somewhat unusual set of facts.

Bunky's mother had a long-time employee who had, for years, paid 25 cents a week to a burial insurance company which, in consideration of this unbroken string of payments, had agreed to conduct the funeral of her husband. When the husband died, the widow began making arrangements for the funeral, but the burial insurance company told the bereaved widow that she had to come up with a substantial additional sum of cash for the funeral to go forward as planned. The widow had no money, and believed that her years of paying 25 cents a week was all that was required. Totally frustrated, she sought the return of her husband's mortal remains so that she could make other – now desperately needed – arrangements.

This was all dutifully recited in Bunky's application for an "Extraordinary Writ" by which he sought return of the mortal remains. The lawyer for the funeral parlor and its affiliated burial insurance company appeared before Honorable Frank Stich of Civil District Court in Orleans and cooly informed the judge that there was no such thing in the law of Louisiana as an Extraordinary Writ.

"There is now," said Judge Stich, as a cheer rose from the audience to applaud Bunky for his noble efforts.

Tom Pugh, a legendary figure on the Baton Rouge legal scene for many years, served as a prosecutor, city court judge and family court judge. Stories about him in each of those capacities abound. Here is a sampling:

As a family court judge, Tom presided over, and rendered the final judgment dissolving a marriage between a fairly young couple. As the couple walked out, they met at the railing between the bar and the audience, looked at each other, and kissed goodbye warmly. Tom's comment from the bench: "That's what I call ending a marriage with a flair."

Michael Bordelon of Mandeville provides this Tom Pugh story:

In 1974, LSU law students were required to spend at least one hour attending a trial. Complying with the requirement, I wandered into Judge Tom Pugh's division of Family Court in the old Baton Rouge courthouse during divorce confirmations.

Judge Pugh had very weak eyesight, which necessitated that he be within a foot of whatever he was trying to see clearly. Consequently, while in Court he routinely rotated his swivel chair to the rear with his back to the courtroom, propped his shoes against the rear wall and, crossing his hands behind his head, leaned backwards on his desk and listened to the testimony.

In one default confirmation, after the spouse testified that she did not have sex with her husband for six months, the attorney called the second corroborating witness to the stand. The witness was a luscious and statuesque woman wearing, in the fashion of the day, a short, tight, sheer, white, strapless dress (and no apparent undergarments). No sound save breathing was heard from the gallery while the attorney asked his questions. When done, he tendered the witness to the Judge.

Judge Pugh dropped his feet from the wall, spun around in his chair and leaned over the box so as to address the witness, placing his face at his customary distance to see her, and so close to her bosom that, some said, his nose was in her cleavage. I swear that I saw his eyebrows flutter when his eyes finally focused. He looked at her for as long as it took, I suppose, while she adjusted her position in the chair, apparently trying to help the poor judge see whatever it was he (and every other person) was looking at.

He straightened in his chair and announced that he had only one question for the witness: "How do you keep that dress up?"

In the early period of Pugh's tenure as City Judge, the vagrancy laws were still in effect – it was a crime if you had no visible means of support. Pugh did not much believe in the vagrancy laws, which was why it was his time of greatest freedom. When the characters rounded up under this charge came before him each week, it was really "show time." If they were before him each week it was really show time. If they were successful at telling the Judge an amusing story, no matter how bizarre, the chances of a lighter sentence were almost assured.

It was in this setting that "Jesus Christ" made his appearance before Judge Pugh. This "Jesus" attempted to affect the appearance of his chosen namesake. After announcing his name to the Judge, there followed a conversation between defendant and the bench that had the entire courtroom convulsed with laughter. The thrust of the examination was the Judge's questioning whether the defendant believed himself to be the Jesus of Biblical history or a namesake. The defendant staunchly insisted his identity as the real thing, and that he was going to New Orleans just prior to Mardi Gras to put a stop to that "Devil's Party."

When finally asked if he had any money, "Jesus" said that he did not, but that his father in heaven always provided for him. Whereupon the judge took a $5.00 bill, gave it to an officer, and told him to put defendant on the next bus to New Orleans. The judge then turned to the defendant and said, "I do not wish to end up in history known as 'Pontius Pugh,' so please continue your journey as my guest."

Judge John Duhé, who has served as a state district judge and federal district judge and a federal court of appeals judge, reminisces about Judge S.O. Landry, who was the resident Iberia Parish judge when John began practicing law. As he tells it:

> Judge Landry was a wise man who humanized the entire judicial experience to the benefit of the bar and the litigants (even if, with his humor, he did take a little hide off lawyers once in a while). He made the ordinary people at home in the courtroom. He never wore a robe and never sat on the bench (always next to the reporter, which put everyone on the same level with him, except the witness and the jurors, who were higher than he was). He always appeared a few minutes before court

began and shook hands with all the lawyers (and some of the litigants, if he knew them). He would tell jokes, and tease the lawyers, especially new lawyers and those from New Orleans. Once I appeared wearing a sport coat rather than a suit. The coat, I must admit, was a little loud, the kind that Allen Smith likes to wear, but not nearly so expensive. After court was in session and I rose to announce that I was ready for trial, Judge Landry cut me off, saying: "Duhé, do you know where you are?" Unable to fathom the real inquiry that lay behind that question, I responded with the obvious: "Yes, Your Honor, I'm in the 16th Judicial District Court, Parish of Iberia, the Honorable S. O. Landry, Judge presiding." He replied: "Well, you are dressed like you think you are at the race track!" I took no offense. It was just his way of leveling the playing field. My opponent was an even less experienced lawyer than I, was from out of the district, and was appearing in his very first case.

Judge Landry used a variation of that on others when from time to time a lawyer appeared wearing a sport coat. The Judge would ask: "Mr. A., which wore out first, the coat or the pants?"

New Orleans lawyers who came out to the "country" during the summer always got in trouble with the judge if they were wearing white or seersucker suits. As they strode confidently down the long aisle from the main door of the court room to the bench (New Orleans lawyers always strode confidently, according to the Judge, because they thought they were coming to the country to teach us country boys how to try lawsuits), Judge Landry would proclaim loudly to the assembled audience: "You see that fellow; he's a city lawyer! You can tell because he's got one of those funny looking city suits!"

"City lawyers" often found themselves in trouble in St. Martin Parish too. Back in the "dark ages" (when I entered the profession), witnesses in St. Martin Parish litigation would frequently lapse into French during their testimony. Since all the local folks in the courtroom spoke French, no one would take notice, except, of course, the out-of-towner who could not speak French. He would usually register an apologetic objection; the judge would grumble about "*@%&#* city lawyers," and send down for the Clerk of Court who would then act as translator.

Justice Jeff Victory of the Louisiana Supreme Court has this memory about Judge C. J. (Neal) Bolin. It seems that the judge kept cartoons about the legal system on his office walls. A favorite of many showed an elderly judge on the bench looking down through his glasses at a young hippie with hair past his shoulders and saying: "Young man, there is not a scintilla of evidence against you in this case – but it just wouldn't be right to let you go."

Judge Charley Holcomb, for many years a trial lawyer and a district attorney, spent his later years on the district bench in Baton Rouge, serving mainly in criminal court. In his later years, his hearing and patience declined, producing some interesting occurrences. At one trial, conviction and sentence of a woman for assaulting a neighbor had just concluded when the defendant muttered a few words that the judge partially heard. Judge Holcomb bellowed: "What is that you said? If it is what I think you said then you are about to see the inside of our jail house!"

She looked at him dead in the eye and clearly and very distinctly replied, saying each word carefully and slowly: "I said, 'Gaud am de judge'."

At an arraignment one day, a lady of the night was brought before Judge Holcomb to plead to charges of prostitution. She was asked her name and where she lived. She said very quietly her name and that she lived in Tangipahoa. The judge looked at her with a puzzled expression on his face and asked, "A tang whore? What kind is that?"

Sleeping judges present a problem, particularly in a bench trial. Here's how one lawyer solved it.

One of our local judges had a habit of taking a little nap after lunch. Some times he would doze off in court during the trial of a case. In one rather serious case involving a building collapse in which the trial lasted for many days, his "napping" became a regular occurrence. At a crucial stage of the trial, when an important expert witness was testifying, the judge, after lunch, proceeded to doze off. Most of us younger lawyers in the case were upset because we felt like the judge needed to hear this witness, who was the key witness in the case. An older lawyer, who happened to be a classmate of the judge and knew him well, solved the problem. He picked up a large stack of law books which were on the counsel table and dropped them on the floor with a resounding crash. The judge woke with a start and a red face. He listened to the witness, and somehow managed to stay awake during the remainder of the trial.

John Lanier
Thibodaux

The following story may be apocryphal, but it certainly could have happened. In a criminal trial in a small community, the prosecuting attorney called his first witness, an elderly woman. He asked if she knew him, and she responded that she had known him since he was a small boy, and that he was a "disappointment" to her because he cheated people, manipulated them, and "talked about them behind their backs."

Taken aback, the prosecutor asked the witness if she knew the defense attorney. Her response: "Yes. I baby-sat for him and he also is a disappointment to me; he's lazy and drinks too much and can't keep a wife."

At this point, the judge called the lawyers to the bench and issued an ultimatum: "If either of you asks her if she knows me, you're in contempt."

In the 1940s in rural north Louisiana, legal proceedings were underway in the second-story courtroom of the stately parish courthouse. The judge, district attorney, and clerk of court were distinguished, experienced gentlemen, each firmly rooted in his own ways, and having an aggregate age approaching 200 years. During the proceedings and upon realization that a public document situated in the clerk of court's office on the first floor was needed, the district attorney impatiently and authoritatively instructed the clerk to retrieve the document from his office. The clerk responded indignantly and impolitely, telling the prosecutor in no uncertain terms that he could go down and get the document himself. The district attorney simply increased the volume and urgency of his instruction to the clerk to go get the document. The clerk, unaffected by the great power of the district attorney, said, "You can go and get your own damn document." The district attorney then turned to the judge and requested that the judge order the clerk of court to retrieve the document. The judge, in an uncomfortable, no-win situation, very courteously stated: "Mr. Clerk, would you please go to your office and retrieve the requested document?" The clerk, yielding to the power of the court, with great reluctance stood and as he was leaving the courtroom gruffly stated, "This is the goddamdest court I have ever seen." The district attorney, now incensed at the actions of the clerk and amazed that the judge did not take action which he deemed appropriate, impatiently asked the judge: "Judge, aren't you going to hold the clerk in contempt for his statement?" The judge thought for a moment and calmly responded: "No, I'm not; I've thought about what he said and I think he may be right."

6. The Chef is in The Courtroom: "Home Cooking"

Every lawyer knows the value of "home cooking," i.e., the favoritism which judges sometimes show toward the folks who elect them. Here is a menu:

A. Appetizers

One time I was trying a case before a judge in another parish involving a local's claim against a funeral home. I asked one of my all time famous leading questions and one of the defense attorneys, a classmate of mine who was defending the funeral home, jumped up and objected to the form of my question. The judge looked over at him and said, "Now, Mr. X, we don't need any of that in this courtroom. We all know we're just here to figure out who owes this family some money and how much." That was the best ruling on an objection I ever heard.

Later, my wife and partner Beth was appearing before the same judge in a domestic matter. Rather than hearing the case in the courtroom, he went into his library with all of the parties. Beth put on her testimony and the judge ruled that there would be a judgment in favor of the plaintiff. The defendant's attorney spoke up and asked: "Judge, can I put on my case before you rule?" The judge responded, "Well, you can, but the plaintiff is still going to win."

Bob Thomas
Lake Charles

B.   The Main Course

Vance Andrus of Lafayette provides two of the best "Home Cooking" stories, one of which is spiced with a vignette on one of southwest Louisiana's greatest lawyers.

After law school, I had the great fortune to clerk for Louisiana Supreme Court Justice Al Tate, known to all as a wise, funny and compassionate man. On several occasions I heard him muttering about "home cooking" as he reviewed trial transcripts. Now, Judge Tate wasn't particularly opposed to the concept, especially when the local judge had his heart in the right place. He noted for me, however, that recognizing home cooking was important in understanding the true underlying principles involved in a decision. Little did I know that just three months after my clerkship I would be subjected to a good dose of it.

The action happened in a small North Louisiana

parish. Two of my classmates and I were hired to represent the interests of an almost defunct little oil and gas company which had been made a defendant in a declaratory judgment suit brought by a large coal company which was interested in building the first lignite (a type of soft coal) plant in North Louisiana. The legal question was simply enough stated:

"Does an antecedent oil and gas lease (giving the lessee the right to explore for and produce "oil, gas and all other minerals") prime a subsequent lignite coal lease?"

The answer, of course, had to be: "No!" If it were otherwise, then all of the citizens and voters of the parish were stuck with their old oil and gas leases, and would be denied the opportunity to lease their lands a second time. However, not realizing that the district judge would make it his "sacred duty" to protect the economic interests of his voters, we went to court blithely assuming we had a chance.

Trial day came and the courtroom was packed with voters, ...err "citizens." The judge was a towering presence with a booming voice and thick silver hair. He ascended the bench and addressed our opponent, an "old school" energy attorney from a first class Shreveport law firm:

"Mr. Carmody, are you ready to proceed?"

"Yes, sir," he replied.

"All right then," said the judge, and turning to us, inquired, "What about you boys?"

Well for the next three days, I was "Boy" and my partner, Todd, was "Son." In fact as the trial wore on we took to referring to each other with those names.

I rose first and requested the

sequestration of the witnesses. Turning, the judge inquired:

"Mr. Carmody, are any of these good people your witnesses?"

"Well," said Mr. Carmody, "Judge, I might need some or all of them."

"Do you think it'll be necessary for me to sequester them?"

"No sir."

"Request denied."

Now this being the first time in my life I had a motion denied (it being my first trial and all), I didn't realize one of the principal rules of trial practice: "Leave bad enough alone!" No, not me, so I said.

"Your Honor, I'm reading here from the Code of Civil Procedure and it says 'and upon the request of a party, shall be sequestered! Not may your honor, shall!"

"Now look here, Boy" said the suddenly perturbed judge. "Are you accusing the fine citizens of this Parish of being dishonest? Now, I've made my ruling; let's get on with it."

And so it went, constantly, for three days. When the plaintiff's geologist began to describe the Dolet Hills, Todd objected that no foundation had been laid.

"Now listen here Son," said the judge. "Everyone around here knows where the Dolet Hills are, and what they look like. If you don't, then maybe at lunch you can get on your motorcycle and ride out there and take a look for yourself." (Did I happen to mention that this was in 1972 and the judge didn't take kindly to our long hair, and worse, facial hair?)

On the third day, the plaintiff introduced his last, and surprise witness, who was none other than Professor George Hardy, formerly of the LSU Law School and the "Reporter" for the Louisiana Mineral Code. We were told that Hardy would offer his expert opinion on the structure and significance of various phrases in the oil and gas lease, as well as the obvious intent of the original parties thereto, none of whom were available to testify.

Although Todd begged me to make the objection, I refused and told him that I had taken enough beatings, and that it was his turn. With the look of a whipped dog, he arose and objected that this was a Louisiana courtroom, for God's sake, and that the judge was the expert on the law, not Hardy.

To this the Judge replied:

"Son, let me tell you something. If I was fortunate enough to have a man with as much talent as Professor Hardy here..."

"Just call me George" said Hardy impishly.

"George here living in this town, you know what I'd do at the conclusion of this case. I'd call him and ask him his opinion, that's what."

"Thank you" said George.

"You're welcome. And another thing, at least you're going to have an opportunity to cross-examine him."

Well, you can probably guess how it

came out. That's right, we lost. You can look it up. It's called Somebody versus "River Rouge Minerals." But if you get a copy of the transcript, don't expect to find <u>any</u> of this. You see, the judge apparently had another little rule. Every time he started talking, the court reporter would take a break in transcribing.

Here is Andrus' second home-cooking story:

This time it was going to be different, I told myself. "Yes, sir, I've got the plaintiff," I thought, and in one way that was true. Only we, my opponent and I, <u>each</u> had a plaintiff; our clients had each sued the other over a wreck that happened late at night on the middle of a bridge spanning a swamp.

This was no ordinary wreck, and my opponent no ordinary attorney. The undisputed point of impact between my client's pickup and his client's pipe truck was directly on the white line in the center of the bridge. The unusual thing was that the vehicles hit right side to right side: passenger door to passenger door. Obviously they were each in the other's lane at the moment of impact, and the question was "Why?"

My opponent was Seth Lewis, a legend of the bar. Small of stature and smart as a whip, he was a courtroom magician. Arrogant, mean, tough, and treacherous, he tried to dominate the courtroom. Others were afraid of him, but not me. I found him fascinating, coiled like a mongoose, always ready to strike with blinding speed and incredible verbal violence.

Seth had developed a move he used on opposing witnesses which was something else. He called it the "Righteous Indignation Hammerlock," and it was every bit as spectacular as anything you've ever seen in pro wrestling. Seth would defer his cross-examination of the opponent until the end of the plaintiff's case in chief. Relieved of the horror of having him pound on your first witness, the plaintiff, you'd relax as your case unfolded, virtually unopposed by Seth. "Virtually" but not "completely" unopposed, because the whole time Seth was introducing, but not highlighting, those little inconsistencies which occur in nearly every trial – a police report slightly at odds with your version, or a witness who didn't see, or could not have seen, some thing. Little blemishes in your case that in your relaxed state you'd misconstrue as beauty marks.

Finally, it would be Seth's turn. He had a remarkable voice, one which was mid-range in pleasant conversation but could rise up in shrill, nasal power and pitch when indignant until it was basically like listening to a skill saw at close range. He'd start slow, letting your client ease into the story, never interrupting and never confronting him. Seth would let the witness re-tell the whole story any way the witness wanted to. Of course, the witness, having heard all of the little inconsistencies, would this time clean up the story. Satisfied with himself, the witness would relax, totally oblivious to the fact that his second sworn version of the event had drifted considerably away from the first. Then with stunning speed and power, Seth would strike. His voice rising in anger and righteous indignation, Seth would slowly rise, all the time posing the question: "Do you expect this Court to believe ... (pregnant pause) to believe your latest version of this event when ..."

Here would follow a comprehensive, argumentative, one-sided listing of every blemish, wart, contradiction, and opposing piece of evidence in the record, all offered up by Seth in his high pitched staccato machine-gun style. Seth then would stand there, jaw jutting out, daring your client to strike back.

Since the question was rhetorical, Seth didn't care if the answer was "yes" or "no," and he didn't care if you objected. There it was, he told me once, stinking up the whole courtroom.

Well, I'd seen him pull that move before, and had seen the results, but I wasn't afraid of him. I was young and smart and brash and relished "going after it" with the old goat (who was probably all of about 56, which, at twice my age then seemed old). Besides, I had a smart, tough client who wouldn't let Seth bait him.

The parish had two sitting judges, and we got the "old man." He really was old and, for all practical purposes, deaf. He did alright in the quiet of his chambers, but in the high chambered courtroom, with its terrible acoustics, he was as deaf as a stone.

This apparent disability didn't bother him, though, and he took the bench daily. About the only time it caused a problem was when one of the attorneys, oblivious of an unwritten local rule, arose and objected to a question. In that parish, objections were considered at least bad form, if not absolutely rude. Why would you object to the orderly flow of evidence, admissible or otherwise, when the objection couldn't possibly affect the outcome of the case? The reason it couldn't possibly affect the outcome was because of the ultimate arbiter of all parish disputes: "The Rules of Home Cooking." Loosely translated, it went like this: "There's us and there's them. We win, they lose."

The distinction between "us" and "them" could be surprisingly flexible. Clearly a resident of the parish was "us," and a Texas oil company was "them." In other instances, having a local attorney alone could qualify one as an "us." Being related to any person employed by any branch of the parish government, especially a Sheriff's deputy or school bus driver, also qualified. Over the years attorneys practicing there, secure in the knowledge that all outcomes were preordained, gradually abandoned the use of objections.

The first day of trial started smoothly enough. Since we both knew the judge couldn't hear us, Seth and I mutually agreed that he could postpone his cross-exam of my plaintiff, and we dutifully dictated a stipulation into the record; the judge, all the while, acted as if he really could hear us.

Now it may seem strange to consider two grown men pretending to try a case to a judge who is pretending to hear it, but that's what we did. Not only that, but we fought like wild animals, joyous in the presence of a worthy adversary. Word went out that we were going after each other with hammer and tong, and by the end of the second day, the courtroom was full. Lawyers, clerks, deputies, they all came, for this was the arena, and Seth and I were going toe to toe.

On the last day of trial, three remarkable things happened. The first involved the judge, the second, Seth, and the third, all three of us.

First, as the day wore on, I noticed that the judge was drifting away. I'm not talking about boredom, nor even exhaustion. It was something else, a vacant look in his eyes that puzzled me. He looked healthy and amiable enough, so I wondered what was wrong. Suddenly, it hit me. I realized that, for the first time in anyone's memory, the Rule of Home Cooking didn't apply. Neither of our clients was from the parish, and further, neither were the lawyers. Since the Rule of Home Cooking didn't apply, the judge was disinterested. He had the look of a man who was called upon to listen to a legal argument between two intergalactic space travelers, spoken in an unknown language and based upon an absent code of law.

The second remarkable thing happened to Seth. He got popped!

There he was, leading my man down

the primrose path.

"Tell us again, Mr. _____, how did it happen?"

"Well, it was late, about 11:30. I had been up since early morning and been traveling round, first to my farm, then to my ranch, and then on to other matters. About 9 p.m., I stopped at a bar and restaurant and, well, I'll admit, I had two beers, but I also had supper, visited with friends, and then left heading west on the highway."

"I was in my lane as I got on to the bridge over the Swamp. As I approached the middle of the bridge, I saw your client's truck slowly start sliding over the center line, coming at me fast. I guess he'd fallen asleep at the wheel. I had no place to go, so I cut it hard to the left and 'bang' we hit at the center of the bridge."

Seth cut his eyes over at me, and with a thin smile started to rise. "Do you expect this Court to believe that version of your story when ..."

And off he went, full of sound and fury, pounding my man mercilessly on a variety of small inconsistencies. He finished, standing there with his jaw out. But a strange thing happened – my witness popped back an answer so fast it made Seth's head spin.

"Why not?" he said. "That's the exact story your client is going to tell."

Seth looked like a caged lion, for the

response was true. My client, who was unconscious after the wreck and had given no statement to the police, had just parroted the statement of Seth's client, changing only the direction of travel. Either that, or Seth's client was a liar who was fortunate enough to be able to get his statement on the police record first. Either way, Seth was stuck in his own Hammerlock. Incensed, he cried out in a loud voice that the answer was not responsive because it contained neither a "yes" or a "no," and he moved to strike the answer.

The only problem was the second thing, the one which didn't happen. The judge didn't respond. He apparently hadn't heard the question or the answer or the objection, and anyway, what were these "extraterrestrials" doing in his courtroom?

The judge may not have heard, but the entire courtroom did, and the audience, having anticipated that this thing might blow up, was laughing aloud. Seth, now desperate, demanded that I stipulate that the answer was non-responsive and that it should br stricken. Realizing the existential absurdity of our predicament, as well as Seth's wrath, I started laughing and refused. "Oh, no, you don't Seth," I said. "This record's going up on appeal with that in it. You grew it, you chew it."

From there, the trial wrapped up quickly. Seth put his man on, and as expected, his testimony sounded like an echo, a mirror image of my client's. At the conclusion of the trial, the judge requested that we stay and await his judgment. This was a violation of another unwritten rule in that parish: out-of-parish attorneys were allowed to leave town with their clients and their dignity intact, with justice swiftly to follow.

As we waited, a succession of onlookers were called in to his office, perhaps to give the judge his or her analysis of the fight. Finally, the judge took the bench. He addressed me first: "Stick, (although my nickname was Twig, he often confused me with my brother), the Code of Civil Procedure provides that in order for you to prevail, you, as plaintiff, must carry your burden of proof by a preponderance of the evidence. This you have failed to do."

Turning to Seth, he said: "Seth, as a plaintiff-in-reconvention, your client is under the same burden. Likewise, you have failed to convince me by a preponderance of the evidence that your client's version is true."

"It is the decision of the Court, therefore, that the plaintiff's demand be dismissed with prejudice, and the plaintiff-in-reconvention's demand be dismissed with prejudice." With that, he wished us a good day, and departed.

Stunned, we both just sat there, as the irony of it all washed over us. After all, what had we accomplished, besides denying each other victory? After a few moments, Seth started to laugh. He had a maniacal cackle for a laugh, and when it started, it started at his toes and exited from the top of his head. He laughed so hard and long that tears came to his eyes, and when he finally finished he walked over, shook my hand and said, "Well, son, I guess we gave'em one helluva show."

C.   The Side Dish

In the late 1950s a young lawyer from Baton Rouge traveled to Covington to try a contract case between his Baton Rouge client and a St. Tammany resident who had failed to pay the sum allegedly due under the contract. His first indication that something was amiss was when the judge suggested that the young lawyer was "missing something." When the young lawyer inquired further, the judge asked if the young lawyer had local counsel. The young lawyer answered in the negative, and the trial began. The young lawyer's first witness was his client's employee, who would identify the contract in suit. He asked the usual question: "I hand you a document and ask if you can identify it?" Then, in rapid fire, came two responses: defense counsel said "I object," and the judge said "Sustained." The young lawyer turned to the judge and asked if he could be advised of the basis of the objection. The judge's response: "Young man, I've known _____ (defense counsel) for many years, and he's made many objections. Some of them were good and some were not. That one was good. Proceed."

After a few seconds elapsed, the young lawyer overcame the "stun" and asked the court reporter if the judge's ruling had been taken down. The judge instructed the court reporter not to record or transcribe the judge's explanation of the ruling. The young lawyer, gaining confidence from combat, told the judge, "Your Honor, you can do anything in this courtroom except falsify the record." The judge looked at the lawyer, whirled around in his chair, announced that the court would be at recess, and stormed off the bench.

The young lawyer felt certain that the judge had taken a recess to determine the heaviest possible penalty for contempt, but he knew at least that his client would be impressed with his valor. He turned away from the bench in time to see his client tip-toeing out the back door of the courtroom. At that point the young lawyer learned the ultimate attorney wisdom: "if somebody on your side has got to go to jail, make damned sure it's your client."

All ended well, however. The judge returned to the bench, granted a continuance and transferred the case to another division, where the young lawyer subsequently obtained a judgment.

D.   The (Just?) Dessert

Judge John Duhé offers this tale:

My primary fault as a lawyer probably was that I overprepared everything. Of course, in this particular case, there was not much to overprepare. I had never appeared in court in the unnamed parish, however, so I thought it best that I obtain a copy of the local rules. I called the clerk's office and told the lady who answered the phone that I would like to have a copy of the court rules. She responded: "Mais cher, you gotta talk with da clerk." I assured her that I didn't think it was necessary, as all I wanted was for someone to mail me a copy of the court rules, but she insisted. Presently the clerk of court himself was on the line and I explained to him that I had a case coming up for trial in about a month before Judge _____, and that I wanted to study the rules of court before I appeared since I had not tried a case there. His response was: "Son, you got to talk to the judge." No matter how I explained to him the simplicity of my request, he remained adamant that it could only be fulfilled by talking with the judge (absolutely the last person I wanted to speak with at this point).

Seeing no other way, I called the judge's office and explained to his secretary that I was a young lawyer practicing in New Iberia, that I was scheduled to try a case before the judge in about a month, and that I was simply looking for a copy of the local rules of court so that I could be familiar with them before I appeared. I apologized for having to disturb her with such a simple request, but advised that I was only doing what the clerk of court had instructed me to do. She listened patiently and then she said: "Just a minute, you have to talk to the judge." Now I was really concerned. I did not want to talk to the judge. I had never spoken to the judge in my life and did not want to trouble him with such a trivial matter. Why was it so difficult to get a copy of the local rules of court in that parish? Before I could hang up the telephone, however, the judge himself was on the line.

I apologized profusely that he had been disturbed by such a simple request, I explained to him who I was, where I was and what I wanted, and I apologized again. Whereupon the judge said: "Well son, exactly what is it you want to know?" I hurriedly explained again that I simply wanted to familiarize myself with all the local rules of his court before I made my initial appearance so that I could comply with those rules and avoid embarrassment to myself. Then I learned the lesson. The judge said, "Well son, they're not exactly written down."

CHAPTER VII

THE WITNESSES

Most depositions and trial testimonies are straightforward "question and answer" sessions which tend to dull the senses of the audience, and, in some cases, the participants. Every now and then, however, a funny moment arises, often because the witness is unsophisticated, nervous or antagonistic. This chapter deals with some of those moments.

1. Out of the Mouths of Babes

Boudreaux injured his arm when his outboard motor flipped into his bateau as he was speeding along Lake Palourde near Morgan City. Boudreaux sued the motor manufacturer, claiming various defects in its construction. It became necessary to put into evidence the information that Boudreaux had received when he bought the motor at a local marine dealer. For this purpose, Boudreaux's lawyer called "Uncle" Leo to the stand. Leo, a voluble Cajun of a certain age who supported himself by engaging in the almost-lost art of moss picking, held forth at great length about what transpired between the marine dealer and Boudreaux. On cross-examination, the following exchange took place:

Q: Now Uncle Leo, you told us all about what the dealer told Boudreaux when he bought that motor?

A: Yes, and that's the truth, too, I want to tell you.

Q: Did you go with Boudreaux when he bought the motor?

A: Well, no.

Q: Isn't that shop in Gonzales?

A: Sure is.

Q: Well then, everything you've told us is an assumption?

A: No, it's not!

Q: It's not an assumption?

A: Of course not. Everybody knows Gonzales is in Ascension, not Assumption!

C. G. "Woody" Norwood
New Orleans

When I was a young lawyer, I often was sent by my senior partners to neighboring Evangeline Parish to try cases for our insurance clients. On one such occasion, I was contesting against my good friend, Preston Aucoin, who later became a judge. At the time, Aucoin was a capable, though somewhat flamboyant, trial attorney. Upon my arrival at the courtroom, I was informed by my opponent and the presiding judge that the plaintiff neither spoke nor understood the English language. Assuming that I neither spoke nor understood French, the judge offered to act as an interpreter during the trial. Being from Avoyelles Parish, I understand French and, if pushed can be conversant in it to a degree. I elected to keep this fact to myself and consented to the judge's offer. After Preston's direct examination, duly interpreted for me by the judge, I opened my cross with this question: "Mr. _____, it is my understanding that you neither speak nor understand the English language, is that correct?" Before the judge could pose my question in French, the plaintiff answered in perfect English, "yes, that's correct."

Jimmy Dauzat
Opelousas

Several years ago when many old Cajuns spoke mostly French, Red Stafford and I were trying a case in

Marksville. My client was more comfortable speaking French, so for Red's benefit, Judge Earl Edwards would interpret the questions and the witness' responses. Red asked a fairly detailed question of the client who, being a Cajun, began a long narration that lasted at least three or four minutes. After the long narration, Judge Edwards looked to Red and said, "In answer to your question, the answer is No."

Chris Roy
Alexandria

Maxwell Bordelon, Sr., generally sent his clients copies of their petitions. On one occasion, Bordelon asked his client (whom we'll call Boudreaux) if he had suffered because of the injury. "Oh, yeah" said Boudreaux, "I suffer a lot." Not satisfied, Maxwell went further and said "how much?" Immediately Boudreaux removed the petition from his coat pocket and declared loudly, "tin tousand dollars wort. ("Old Cajuns could not pronounce "th's", thus the "tin tousand dollars wort.")

Chris Roy
Alexandria

The wife was petitioning the court for interdiction of her husband. Counsel was asking the requisite material questions, concluding with "Has your husband lost effective use of his senses?" The reply was, "No sir, he never had no sense." And finally, "Is your husband able to manage his affairs?" "No sir, at his age he can't manage me, much less no other woman."

Terminology sometimes trips up the witness. In an uncontested divorce case, the plaintiff-husband was testifying to the essentials in a divorce on the grounds of adultery. He made several references to the "husband-in-law." When asked to explain the meaning of this title he responded, "The man living with my wife."

Judge Jacques Weiner of New Orleans submits this example of twisted terminology:

> A 1L member of the Tulane Law School class of '61 landed a clerkship for the summer of '59 with a New Orleans insurance defense firm. Tagging along at counsel table in Civil District Court in the course of a trial of an automobile personal injury case, the student listened as his mentor, in cross-examining a middle-aged, uneducated witness for the plaintiff, inquired, "And Madam, what is your relationship to the plaintiff?" The witness paused for quite a while with a querulous look on her face; then, as if a light had turned on, she faced counsel and stated forcefully, "He's my common-law brother-in-law!"

The jury venire was being questioned *en masse* in federal court. The court, in questioning one member of the venire, learned that he could not read and write and, accordingly, excused him. The court then asked the general question, "Is there anyone else who cannot read and write?" One man stood up and said, "I can't, Your Honor." The judge asked the man his name, looked down at his venire list, and then said, "You're not a prospective juror, are you?" The response was, "No, sir, I am a witness, but I can't read and I was hoping you would let me go too."

> Judge Edwin Hunter was sitting on a case in Opelousas in which a trapper was charged with taking ducks after the legal shooting hours. The judge asked him whether he wanted to plead guilty to the charge. His reply was "I don't think I was guilty. I didn't kill any ducks." The judge explained that the crime included the act of hunting after legal shooting hours, whether or not one killed any migratory game bird. Under questioning, the accused admitted he was in a blind, with decoys out in the pond, a retriever in the blind with him, and a loaded shotgun. The judge asked him this question. "You were fully equipped for hunting. Were you hunting or not?" The accused, an uneducated man said, "Well, Judge, you might as well get me for rape too because I was fully

equipped for that." The judge left the bench, went to his chambers and regained his composure before returning to impose sentence.

Judge Richard Putnam
Abbeville

As a JAGC officer in the Army I served as defense counsel for the regular general court martial. Much of my work was defending soldiers accused of desertion. These cases were easy for the prosecutor who simply filed "an extract copy of morning report" attesting that the soldier was absent without leave (AWOL) from and after a certain date. If the soldier was gone long enough, a presumption arose that he did not intend to return to duty and had therefore deserted, a very serious offense. The only meaningful defense was to admit that the soldier was AWOL and try to establish that he did intend to return.

I defended, on a desertion charge, a big, blond, mid-western farm boy who had been arrested at the family farm. Although it was unusual to call these defendants to the stand, I put this defendant on and had him testify that after the unexpected death of his father, he left the Army post and went home to help his mother get the crops planted. Of course, he intended to return when he finished his chores. In an attempt to bolster his credibility, I asked:

Q: Weren't you plowing when the FBI arrested you?

A: No sir.

Q: Are you sure?

A: Yes sir.

Q: (In panic) Didn't you tell me you were sitting on the tractor when the FBI arrested you?

A: Yes sir.

Q: But you weren't plowing?

A: No sir. I was discing.

There must have been some farm boys on the court who knew the difference between plowing and discing, because the soldier readily was found not guilty of desertion.

Judge John Parker
Baton Rouge

Perhaps the most common "faux pas" by a witness at a deposition or at trial – and perhaps an indication of untrustworthiness – is when the witness begins the response to a question with "Don't quote me but ...." Here's a report by Bunky Healy of New Orleans which must have had the opposite effect.

About 35 years ago, I was trying a case in the Western District of Louisiana before Judge Ben C. Dawkins, Jr., representing Vidalia Dock and Storage Company, which had been sued for allegedly permitting Cargill's grain conveyor to collapse and fall in the Mississippi River. Cargill alleged that it had entrusted the care of the conveyor to Vidalia at its fleeting facility just upriver from the Natchez-Vidalia bridge. Vidalia contended that although it had attempted to confect an agreement with Cargill to store Cargill's equipment, Cargill never agreed to the proposition and had in fact moored the equipment about a quarter of a mile upriver from Vidalia's facility. The location of the equipment at the time of the collapse was, obviously, a very crucial issue. One of the witnesses I called to support the proposition that the conveyor belt was not on Vidalia's property when it collapsed was Captain Sonny Boy Smith, the captain of the BETTYE MCGEHEE. We were fortunate to have several aerial photographs, furnished by the United States Corps of Engineers, which were taken a few months prior to the casualty and which depicted the river, levee, batture and adjoining properties. Using a blowup of one of the photographs, I asked Captain Smith to place an

128

X on the photograph where he remembered the equipment was before and after the collapse. He did as instructed. On cross examination by plaintiff's attorney, Smith explained the absence of a ship's log or accident report by noting that he had quit school in the second grade before he learned to read and write. Plaintiff's attorney obviously believed there would be some inconsistency in any written document, but the absence of any writings perplexed him. Later during his cross examination plaintiff's attorney asked Captain Smith to point to the location on the river of the tug BETTYE MCGEHEE. Smith did as requested, whereupon plaintiff attorney asked the witness to place a "Y" at the location of the tug. To everyone's surprise, Captain Smith, with a puzzled look on his face, said to plaintiff's attorney, "How do you make a Y?"

Plaintiff's attorney rose on his toes much like a matador about to plant his sword, and said, "Ah, you had no trouble making a X when Mr. Healy asked you to do so, how come you can't make a Y?" The entire courtroom burst into laughter at Smith's response: "An X is what I use to sign my name."

One of the clearest examples of witness credibility came in an intersectional collision case which I tried in Washington Parish some years ago. The defendant, driving his pulpwood truck, did not yield at a stop sign, but in fact sped up as he reached the intersection of the road on which he was traveling and La. Hwy. 1071, resulting in a collision with the plaintiff. On the stand, defendant told this story: He had driven down a dirt road off La. Hwy. 1071 and parked his truck, with the windows down, in a shaded area while he went fishing. He returned to his truck and was driving back to Hwy. 1071. He had almost reached the intersection when he saw a green snake crawling on his right shoulder.

Beginning his cross-examination, the opposing

lawyer stood up, addressed the defendant and exclaimed, "now let's talk about this alleged snake." The defendant interrupted "Mister, that weren't no ledged snake, it was a green snake." At that point, I advised counsel they could accept as fact there was a green snake.

Judge Hillary (Buddy) Crain
Bogalusa

During a slip and fall case, the only eyewitness was the plaintiff's cute little 10 year-old, redheaded daughter. The plaintiff's attorney questioned her very carefully and deliberately as follows:

Q.   Now, did you go with your mother to the Winn-Dixie?

A.   Yes, sir.

Q.   And, did you follow your mother down the fruit and vegetable aisle?

A.   Yes, sir.

Q.   Did you see what happened to your mother?

A.   Yes, sir.

Q.   And what is it that happened to her?

A.   She fell.

Q.   Did you see what your mother fell on?

A.   Yes, sir.

Q.   And what did she fall on?

A.   Her butt.

Judge Durwood Conque
Abbeville

During a child custody hearing the child's grandmother, a sweet silver-haired lady, was on the witness stand. An objection was made and the lawyers became engaged in a discussion over the merits of the objection. Apparently thinking that the judge needed a little help, the grandmother tapped on the bench and asked, "Would you like to know what Judge Judy would do?"

Judge Durwood Conque
Abbeville

Alec Andrus of Opelousas provides this delightful story about a witness's testimony:

Boudreaux went to Thibodeaux's home to assist Thibodeaux in roof repairs. While Boudreaux was working on the roof, he was struck by a beam being hauled up to the roof, and was injured. While they waited for the ambulance to arrive, Thibodeaux explained this problem to Boudreaux: the beam that struck him was attached to Broussard's truck, Thibodeaux had borrowed the truck from Broussard, who was a nurse at the local hospital and who was recovering from serious mental problems, and that the fear that she would be sued because of the use of her truck might "drive Broussard over the edge." Thibodeaux assured Boudreaux that he had plenty of homeowner's insurance to cover Boudreaux's claim, and that because of these circumstances, Boudreaux should tell everyone that the beam that struck him came from the roof and not from the truck. Boudreaux agreed and told that story at the hospital. Broussard was in attendance at the hospital and heard the story. The insurer filed a claim against Broussard's liability insurer, as the facts revealed that Broussard's truck was the real culprit. At trial, Boudreaux testified on direct examination that his injury was caused by the truck. Subsequently, the insurer put Broussard on the stand, and she related how Boudreaux had told her and everyone else at the hospital on the night of the accident that the offending beam came from the house and not the truck. When Boudreaux returned to the stand, he thereafter reaffirmed the "truck origin" story. On cross examination the insurer's counsel asked him how he came to tell a different story at the hospital. Boudreaux's response was: "Well, the truth is, I lied!"

2.   It's Not So Much What He Said, But the Way He Said It

I once was taking the deposition of an Arkansas man who had fallen into a barge. Despite my best efforts to articulate my questions regarding the depth of the barge, we just were not communicating. Finally, in frustration I asked, "Well sir, how far did you fall? How long did it take you to hit the bottom?"

Using a classic Arkansas drawl, the witness replied, "Well, Mr. Welch, I don't rightly know how far I fell, but I could have read the Bible twice before I hit the bottom."

Hal Welch
New Orleans

At the deposition of a witness to an explosion at one of the chemical plants along the Mississippi River, the witness was asked what he did when he heard the explosion. His response: "I started running away." To the question, "How fast were you running?" He replied, "About medium." Asked what "medium" meant, the deponent said, "I was passing some, and some were passing me."

Professor Tom Richard
Southern University Law Center

Neil Sweeney and I were defending an industrial plant across the river on a claim of environmental damage to a subdivision. We were deposing an older woman who lived near the plant, and she kept saying that she was attending meetings with the Gulf Coast Tenants Association. When we asked what was discussed at the meetings, she said "we all talked about emotions." Well, this went on for some time and Neil and I were puzzled. After another 30 minutes of questioning (we were slow learners) we asked her exactly what emotions were discussed. She responded, "you know, the emotions coming out of the smoke stacks at the plant."

G. William Jarman
Baton Rouge

At a trial the lawyer asked a minister-witness, who was a member of the Southern University Board of Supervisors, whether another member of the board was his good friend. The reverend replied: "Yeah, and Judas was a good friend to Jesus Christ too."

Judge Louis Doherty
Baton Rouge

In a jury trial in Livingston Parish, my client was an elderly lady who hit a roadway flagman while driving her 1967ish LTD sedan to Baton Rouge to have her ophthalmologist repair her detached retina. One of the witnesses to the accident was a telephone company employee who was working in a bucket, suspended above the accident scene. On examination, he admitted that he had not actually seen my client hit the plaintiff. Rather, he said that he heard a thump, looked down, and there, according to him, was the plaintiff, "flying through the air, like Superman, only upside down."

Murphy Burke
Baton Rouge

3. Sex on the Stand

The defendant was on trial for simple assault and theft of money from the victim, who had cashed her check after getting off work and had safeguarded the money, as was her practice, by putting it in her bra. She got off the trolley and, as the evening shadows lengthened, began walking the short distance to her home. Halfway home, she ran into the defendant, someone she obviously knew, who pulled her behind a large oak tree, unbuttoned her blouse, pulled up her bra, took her money and ran off. She called the police, and assault and theft charges resulted. Towards the end of his questioning, the prosecutor asked her if she had made any outcry during the encounter. She responded, "No sir." The prosecutor had a puzzled look on his face when he asked, almost incredulously, "Why didn't you?" Equally incredulous, the witness replied, "Lawyer, I didn't know he was after my money."

In a suit for divorce on the grounds of adultery, the only evidence submitted by the plaintiff wife was a videotape she found in the glove compartment of her husband's pick-up truck. The husband and his paramour had decided to record one of their hot trysts on camera. The action was explicit and certainly x-rated. During the scene, the paramour can be heard to say, "Man, if your wife ever gets a hold of this tape, you are in for it."

Judge Durwood Conque
Abbeville

Legend has it that in a rural, genteel setting in the 1940s or 50s, a rather routine hearing was underway in the courtroom. The prosecutor was an aristocratic attorney, a community leader and in the highest social echelon in the community. The prosecutor called a female witness known to him by name only to testify. To put it mildly, the female witness was from the "other side of the tracks" and certainly not in the social circles of the prosecutor. The witness was very well-endowed with a figure of epic proportions which was enhanced by a dress that hid little of a great cleavage. As she settled into the stand, the prosecutor, perhaps startled by her unforgettable appearance, but also in a somewhat superior tone said: "Well, you are a regular Mae West, aren't you?" Without missing a beat, the witness dramatically responded in her best Mae West voice: "That's right, so why don't you come up and see me some time, big boy?

Judge John D. Crigler
St. Joseph

Defendant was before the court on criminal charges for non-support of an alleged illegitimate child. The mother testified that defendant was the father, but, as was the custom of the district attorney in those days, she was required to produce other witnesses to establish paternity. One of the witnesses, a young man, testified that some time earlier the defendant told him that the defendant was the father of the child at issue. On cross examination, he was asked, "What else did defendant tell you at the time?" The witness' response: "He told me he might be my daddy too."

Cliffe Laborde
Lafayette

A certain domestic case comes before a state district judge about every nine months. The judge wondered why the parties were so viciously angry with one another that they would engage in so much litigation until one of the court hearings brought out some details about their relationship. (We'll call the parties the Smiths). Mr. Smith said one time his wife left the house around 11:00 P.M. and spent the entire night out, riding around with two young men. Her lawyer said, "Isn't this after you two had a fight?" Mr. Smith answered, "Yes, she hit me on the head with a Coca-Cola bottle." Her lawyer inquired further, "Isn't that the Coca-Cola bottle you forced her to have sex with, along with a cucumber?" Mr. Smith looked blankly and said, "I remember the Coc- Cola bottle, but I don't remember the cucumber." When the parties return to court, which is often, the judge still can't look at either of them.

A woman filed a charge in city court against a man for breaking and entering. She testified that they were in a public club where drinking and dancing were taking place. The man danced with her, and then when the music stopped, she left to go to her home, which was situated next door. She stated that, unknown to her, the man followed her. When she went into her house, she locked the door. The man came up and demanded to be permitted to enter. When she refused, he broke in the door.

The man, in defense, stated that while they were dancing, he offered her $5.00 for sexual favors. She took the money and told him to follow her to her home next door, which he did. He stated that when he got to her house, she suddenly slammed the door and locked it and refused to permit him to enter. He stated that he broke the door down and went in merely in an attempt to retrieve the $5.00.

The lady then requested to make a statement in rebuttal. The Court permitted, and she stated, "Your Honor, I am an honorable woman, and if he had given me $5.00 to lay with him, I would have laid with him."

Judge Marcus "Buddy" Broussard
Abbeville

A married individual was sued for paternity. When questioned as to whether or not he had relations with the mother, he answered, "Yes." When asked whether he used any form of birth control, with the mother, who also was married, his response was: "Of course not. It is against my religion."

Alan Fishbein
Baton Rouge

No collection would be complete without the following story, which has variously been reported from several courts around the state.

The charge was in city court and involved a fight, a knife, and a stabbing. The defendant was not represented by counsel, a not-so-unusual situation in city court in the 60s and 70s. The judge had emphasized to the victim the imperative of testifying truthfully. The prosecutor was moving the evidence quickly and doing a bit of leading of the victim, the state's star witness. "You were playing cards with several men?" "Yes sir." "It turned into a shoving match between the two of them?" "Yes sir." "You tried to break it up and push the two apart, then the defendant took out his pocket knife?" "Yes sir." "And you got cut in the fracas?" "No sir." Surprised, the prosecutor raised his voice saying, "You were not cut in the fracas?" After the witness glanced over at the judge, his slow, carefully articulated reply was, "No sir, I got cut twixt the belly button and the fracas."

4. Would You Buy a Used Car From this Witness?

An assistant D.A. with the Nineteenth Judicial District was trying an assault and battery case in which the defendant had beaten someone outside a local establishment after closing time. The two supposed "eyewitnesses" for the defendant each testified that their good friend could not have been the felon in question because all three had left the bar well before the 2 a.m. closing time. The prosecutor asked each witness (the defendant took the Fifth) what time that witness had left the bar. Although the witnesses were sequestered, each testified "12:18 a.m.," with arrival times at home of "12:52 a.m." The prosecutor naturally was interested in the "exactitude and specificity" of their time keeping, so the follow-up question was: "How can you be so sure of the exact time you left the bar and the exact time you arrived at home."

To the great surprise of the prosecutor, each witness answered the same way: "We're all good friends, we hang out together, and we always 'simonize' our watches before any serious partying begins."

Despite their timekeeping abilities, the two friends did not make particularly credible witnesses, and the defendant was convicted.

Larry Roedel
Baton Rouge

After I stated to a witness, "Your testimony is incredible, unbelievable, inconsistent, conflicting, unsubstantiated, uncorroborated, and ridiculous," the witness replied, "Well, I guess I can step down now."

Judge Tony Graphia
Baton Rouge

5. The Experts and "Quasi Experts"

Several years ago, I had a case in which the plaintiff was claiming a number of injuries, including temporomandibular joint dysfunction, better known as TMJ. She had been treated by a local dentist, now deceased. During the course of the dentist's deposition, the following exchange occurred:

Plaintiff's counsel: "Dr._____, can having TMJ affect your sex life?"

Dr._____ : "I dunno....maybe your oral sex life."

Murphy Burke
Baton Rouge

Question to a medical expert, "Doctor, if you had the opportunity to make all the tests needed, would your testimony contain fewer words such as "maybe, possibly, and probably, etc." His answer: "Hopefully."

Judge Tony Graphia
Baton Rouge

The plaintiff claimed that her home had been illegally searched by law enforcement officers looking for an escaped female inmate from Hunt Correctional. This search occurred while plaintiff and her family were out of town on vacation. She claimed to have suffered grievous and diverse injuries, and demanded significant money damages. To support her case, plaintiff called a witness who testified that he was a medical doctor, and he was accepted as an expert. A transcript of his testimony would read something like this:

Mr. Lawyer:

Q: Doctor, did you treat Mrs. _____ ?

A: Yes sir.

Q: Were you able to arrive at a diagnosis of her problems?

A: Yes sir. Diagnosis: violation of Fourth Amendment rights, search of home without a warrant. She suffered great mental anguish.

Q: Did you prescribe a course of treatment for Mrs. _____ ?

A: Yes sir. I prescribed that she be "zonked" out."

The Court:

Q: Doctor, this term "zonked out" that you used, is not familiar to me. Is it a term frequently used in the medical profession?

A: You will not find it in the medical books, Your Honor, but it is a term that we use a lot.

Q: What does "zonked out" mean?

A: I doped her up on drugs and kept her in the hospital for thirty days to calm her down.

Plaintiff was unsuccessful in her quest for damages.

Judge John Parker
Baton Rouge

In a city court case in which the lawyers were scrapping over an electrician's bill of $80.00, an electrician, who had been in court for four days waiting to testify as an expert witness concerning the quality and value of the services, turned to me and said: "Judge, just tell me how much the bill is and I will pay it myself."

Judge Louis Doherty
Baton Rouge

Early in my career I was in City Court in Lake Charles to handle a matter. Presiding was Judge Ralph Hanks, who had a few traffic matters to dispose of before taking up my case. One of these involved a man who was charged with exceeding the speed limit in a 30 MPH zone. The defendant represented himself and his own testimony was unremarkable, but the testimony of the lady who was a passenger in his car was not. She testified emphatically that the car was not going any faster than 26 miles per hour. The testimony then went something like this:

Prosecutor: You say the car was not going any faster than 26 miles per hour. Did you look at the speedometer?

Witness: No sir.

Prosecutor: Then how did you know that the car was going no faster than 26 miles per hour?

Witness:	I can tell how fast we is going by how I bounce on the seat.
Judge Hanks:	Wait a minute. Are you telling this court that you can tell how fast a car is going by how you bounce on the car seat?
Witness:	Oh, yes sir!
Judge Hanks:	(Bouncing up and down in his seat at the bench) How fast am I going now?
Witness:	Oh, about 17 miles an hour.

John B. (Spike) Scofield
Lake Charles

6. Of Woodsheds

Preparing the witness – called "woodshedding" – is a crucial part of trial preparation. The stories below illustrate that "woodshedding" may not be limited to pre-trial meetings and may apply to every aspect of the witness' testimony, and that sometimes you can't "woodshed" enough. Spike Scofield of Lake Charles provides a story in which "woodshedding" could have been afoot.

Over 30 years ago I tried what was probably the first case in Southwest Louisiana in what is now the huge field of environmental law. Daigle v. Continental Oil Company, 277 F. Supp. 875 (W.D. La. 1967). Judge Hunter was the presiding judge. The case involved a suit by a number of people living near the Conoco refinery complaining that emissions from the Conoco carbon black plant had befouled their property and person. After I filed my suit on behalf of a number of landowners in the area, the cases were consolidated for trial. One of the clients was a delightful gentleman named Jessie Arceneaux.

One of the local lawyers defending Conoco was Frank Brame (now retired), who was not only a good lawyer but also was extremely meticulous. Part of Frank's cross examination of Mr. Arceneaux went something like this:

Brame:	Mr. Arceneaux, have you ever eaten jelly beans?
Arceneaux:	Jelly beans. What's that?
Brame:	It's a candy. Jelly beans are oval or cylindrical in shape and each is about one-quarter to one-half inch long. Jelly beans are packaged in plastic or cellophane bags and they come in all different colors – red, green, yellow, black, orange, and so on. Each jelly bean has a rather hard, colored coating and on the inside is a softer, gelatin candy.
Opposing Counsel:	Your Honor, I can't see the relevancy of this questioning.
Judge Hunter:	I tend to agree. Where are you going with this, Mr. Brame?
Brame:	We intend to prove, Your Honor, that the pigmentation used in making black jelly beans is none other

	than carbon black and that the ingestion of carbon is not harmful.
Opposing Counsel:	Could we have a recess, Your Honor?
Judge Hunter:	The court will be in recess for 10 minutes.

(After the recess and the resumption of testimony)

Brame:	Now Mr. Arceneaux, I was describing jelly beans to you when the court called a recess. Do you remember that?
Arceneaux:	Oh, yes sir.
Brame:	Do you like jelly beans?
Arceneaux:	Well, yes sir.... all but them black ones.

There was an elderly lawyer (whom we'll call Tom) practicing in Shreveport in the early 60s who had a reputation for being a very able lawyer who really looked after his client's best interests, going the extra mile plus on some occasions. In one criminal trial, the court had taken a brief afternoon recess after the state rested. Upon returning to the courtroom, it appeared everyone was in place – judge, jury, prosecutor – except the lawyer and his client. The judge asked about their whereabouts and the bailiff responded that he thought they were just outside in the hall with several other people. The judge instructed the bailiff to bring them into the courtroom. The bailiff went outside for just a few seconds and returned to the door of the courtroom and said in a booming voice, "Judge, Mr. Tom says he will be right with you, just as soon as he finishes introducing the defendant to his character witnesses."

A rice farmer from south Louisiana was involved in an accident while engaged in hauling hay on a public highway. After his insurer denied coverage, he hired Frank Maraist (who was then in private practice) to represent him. Maraist met on numerous occasions with the insurance company's attorney and made numerous demands that the company settle within policy limits, all of which were denied. Because he could foresee that he would be a witness in his client's subsequent trial against his insurance company, Maraist transferred the client to me for representation. The matter ultimately went to trial, and I represented the farmer, with whom I had met on several occasions, and, I thought, had prepped and prepared him for his testimony at trial.

All went smoothly until we got to the final portion of his testimony, wherein he would have to prove that he had hired me as his attorney to substantiate our claim for attorney's fees. I put the question to him, "Do you have an attorney in this matter?" This question evidently stunned him, because here was his attorney asking him if he had an attorney. Receiving no reply, I stated, "Mr. _____, am I not your attorney?" To this, after some moments of silence, he mumbled, "Yes." Then I said, "Tell the Court the name of your attorney," at the same time pointing to myself. He replied, "Mark Boudreaux!" At the response, the court broke down in laughter. The presiding judge (the late Charles Everett) nearly fell backwards in his chair laughing. My law partner, who was sitting next to me at the trial, did fall out of his chair with laughter. When Judge Everett finally regained control of himself and the courtroom, he looked at me with laughing eyes and with a huge smile on his face and said, "Mr. Broussard, you may lead your witness." I then led him to state for the record my name and that I was his attorney.

Judge Marcus (Buddy) Broussard
Abbeville

It had been a long and difficult day. One by one, members of the defendant-corporation's board of directors had taken the stand in defense of themselves and their company; each had denied the plaintiff's allegations regarding the substance of a lengthy board meeting at which it was alleged they had conspired against the minority shareholder/member of the board of directors who was the plaintiff.

The plaintiff's lawyer followed the old "never flinch" rule, but he could see that his client was losing his case for an injunction. If only by sheer tenacity, however, the plaintiff was still adamant. Insisting that he be allowed to tell his story, he finally convinced his skeptical lawyer to put him on the stand. His testimony was simplistic and plainly biased, but he became more convinced of its righteousness. As the plaintiff's lawyer became discouraged, his questions grew slower and shorter, but the plaintiff's answers grew longer and more rambling. After several objections to non-responsiveness were sustained, the plaintiff's lawyer approached his client and placed his arm around the witness on the stand. For a few minutes they whispered together furtively. The imperturbable judge sat very close by, but hardly raised an eyebrow at the secret conference.

Back at the defense counsel's table, the senior lawyer asked his junior associate why he did not object, but the second chair was silent. The secret conference ended and the plaintiff's lawyer returned to his table to ask several more questions. Again he approached his client on the stand, put his arm around him, and recommenced the secret whispering. Again defense counsel, in consternation, wondered if he should object and finally blurted out:

Defense Counsel: Your Honor, I object. The witness and his lawyer are whispering in secret in the middle of his testimony. This is highly improper. I object.

The gruff old trial judge looked up and queried:

Judge: Are you telling me that this man can't talk to his lawyer?

Defense Counsel: No, but not in the middle of his testimony, Your Honor, this is highly improper and I object.

Judge: Well, I overrule your objection. You might have a point if the lawyer was telling the witness what to say, but from where I'm sitting, it sounds like the witness is telling the lawyer what to ask.

Steven "Buzz" Durio
Lafayette

Sam D'Amico of Baton Rouge sends this one:

Several years ago a State employee was charged with failure to deposit the full amount of his collections for driver's licenses. His wife called me with reference to representing him. When I mentioned my fee, her response was, "Do you know the number to the Welfare Department?" Subsequently, the court appointed me and another lawyer to represent this fellow – pro bono.

During the trial, the defendant's four year old son sat inside the area reserved for lawyers and within a few feet of the jury box.

The father was called to testify. In a momentary lull, with the jury in the box and the father on the witness stand, the son jumped out of his chair, ran toward his father with arms outstretched and screamed "I want my daddy". Do you need to ask what was the verdict?

(Editor's note: Sam swears there was "no coaching").

7. Necessity is the Father of Fantasy

In the famous "Turkey Baster" paternity case, the man proven to be the father by DNA testing denied sexual intercourse but asserted that while they didn't have sex, the woman did fellate him "to give him some relief," saved his semen, and then inserted it into herself by using a turkey baster.

In another case, the man admitted to sex, but insisted that he had "pulled out in plenty of time" (*coitus interruptus)* and had ejaculated on her stomach, alleging the sperm "must have just jumped in there." You gotta watch those tricky little devils.

Michael Bordelon
Mandeville

8. Turning the Tables

Every trial lawyer has asked a question which he wishes he could take back as the words leave his or her mouth, and probably every participant in the trial process has had a witness' testimony rebound to his personal detriment. Here are a few examples:

Our law firm was engaged to represent a refrigerator truck driver, his employer and its liability insurer in a lawsuit filed by a small town socialite who was seeking damages for a "whiplash" that she allegedly sustained when her vehicle was struck in the rear by the refrigerator truck.

The police report reflected the claimant's version of what had happened. The file material that I was provided by the adjuster revealed that there was damage to the rear of the claimant's vehicle and to the front of the insured's truck. When I interviewed my insured, the truck driver, he said no one would believe what actually happened, i.e., that he was stopped behind the claimant, who had pulled too far into the intersection, and that she backed up quickly into his truck to avoid being struck by an oncoming vehicle. He told me that the "old white fellow" who operates the service station at the intersection saw what happened, but would never come forward because he was a Klan member. The driver would make a good witness, but with the claimant's testimony, the physical evidence, and no one to corroborate his story, he did not have a chance. Yet, his story was not one that I suspected him of making up. I decided to try to check it out.

I drove to the intersection, filled my car up at the service station, paid my bill and asked the elderly operator if I could leave my car parked on the lot while I took some photographs. With his consent, I parked on the lot and began taking pictures of the intersection. I did not think that my plan was working, but he finally approached me, and asked what I was doing. I pulled out a copy of the petition, pointed to the quantum demand and told him I was the lawyer for the truck driver's insurance company.

His face reddened, and he declared that lying people like the claimant are the reason that his insurance premiums were so high. He did not care if she was a "home town girl." He then corroborated the truck driver's version of what had happened.

I gave a copy of his sworn statement to the

claimant's counsel well in advance of trial. He disregarded it, and at trial, he vigorously cross examined the old gentlemen. He confronted him with a number of hypothetical situations – maybe you were blinded by the sun, etc. The gentleman's patience finally wore thin, and he responded to a final supposition with: "Son, you have been watching too damn much television." A verdict for the defendant followed extended laughter throughout the courtroom.

J. D. Cascio
Monroe

My beloved late law partner, Larry Dupuis, always had a sympathetic ear for those down on their luck. Larry had a true calling; indeed he really believed that his primary responsibility was to help those in need and not simply to practice law to make a living. Our partner, Nolan Edwards, would constantly, but in a light hearted manner, remind Larry to collect some fee and court costs in advance before taking on a criminal or domestic relations case.

Once a battered spouse consulted with Larry about representing her to secure temporary custody of her small children, and to remove her estranged spouse from the family home so that she and her children could return there to live. After a lengthy consultation Larry told her: "The first thing you have to do is to leave home, go to your parents' home with your children, and get away from that man until we can go to court and have the judge rule that you are entitled to live in the family home and have the judge order that he must stay away from you."

At the hearing on the Rule to Show Cause Larry put the client on the stand to explain why she left the family home and why she was forced to leave by her husband. He asked her, "what is the very first thing I told you to do before we could go to court and seek relief?" The woman thought momentarily and then answered, "You told me I had to bring you $250.00."

Homer Ed Barousse
Crowley

In a deposition, my good friend Tom Hayes, III was questioning the two plaintiffs (twin sisters) about a particular "watering hole" they operated in the southern section of West Monroe known as Bawcomville. Tom jokingly asked whether the two young ladies had ever seen me in the establishment and they both responded, "No." However , they then volunteered that they had "seen Tom in the bar on more than one occasion."

Tommy Zentner
Monroe

One of the most amusing stories occurred in Opelousas while a judge was on the bench hearing a simple battery case arising out of a fight that took place in one of the town's bordellos. The "madam" operating the house of ill repute was testifying and the question arose as to which side of the door the piano was situated. The madam was asked the question and replied, "I can't remember". She then looked up at the judge and said, "Judge, which side of the door is the piano?" That about ended the case.

Judge Richard Putnam
Abbeville

In a minority shareholder's suit, the employee had been called to the stand by the defendant-majority shareholder, his employer. A long time had passed since the conversations the employee was supposed to have witnessed, but his employer had little else to contradict the plaintiff. Direct examination was straightforward and simple; the employee remembered things exactly the way his boss had. In fact, there was a truly remarkable correspondence between his testimony and that of the defendant-employer.

Cross-examination began rapidly as the employee was confronted with inconsistencies between his direct testimony at trial and his previous deposition. While the employee acknowledged there was a difference in his testimony, he claimed to have been "confused" at the time of his deposition. Impeached again, the employee again said he must have been confused. Finally, he was confronted with the most serious discrepancy, and was asked, rhetorically, "Were you confused again?" A faint smile appeared, he nodded frankly, and with evident relief responded, "Mister, I stay confused." Judging by the hearty laughter, the jury evidently found this last testimony convincing. Of course, the plaintiff's lawyer thanked the witness and asked no further questions.

Steven "Buzz" Durio
Lafayette

9. Some Unusual Depositions

Every older lawyer has an "unusual deposition" story. Here are three of the best:

Counsel scheduled the plaintiff's deposition in Houston where he was living when suit was filed. Unbeknownst to counsel, plaintiff had moved to Baton Rouge when his attorney wrote instructing him to be at a certain place in Houston at a certain date and time for the taking of his testimony. They had no other communication relative to the deposition. On the appointed day, both plaintiff and defense counsel and a court reporter arrived at the airport for the flight to Houston, and were flabbergasted to find that the plaintiff was already there, booked on the same flight. After some consultation, all four boarded the flight, flew to Houston, took the deposition, and returned home. How's that for accommodation?

Gerry Covert
Baton Rouge

Years ago, when my oldest son was a teenager, I had a duck lease in the western part of the state. One day I had an early morning deposition in a town which happened to be exactly halfway between my home and my duck lease. The deposition was set on a day when my son did not have school. I asked if he wanted to go duck hunting and attend the deposition, thinking that he would really enjoy the duck hunt and be impressed by my legal skills. He readily agreed.

My client was a young lady who, while minding her own business sitting on a bar stool in the town lounge, was forcibly struck in the face by another patron. The perpetrator of this ungentlemanly act had been fighting with his father. The deponent on the morning of the duck hunt was another defendant who was not only the bartender that night but the owner of the bar as well.

As I recall, we had a so-so duck hunt. We arrived at the bar where the deposition was to be held. Everybody was there. I began questioning the bartender about the nature of the dispute between the father and the son, carefully demonstrating that it should have been evident to him before the first blow was struck that there would be fight and that he had done nothing to stop it. I asked the bartender to recite in graphic details the events immediately preceding the blow to my client. I inquired what the patron did just before he hit my client. He answered: "He was wrestling on the floor with his father." With false surprise, I exclaimed: "He was wrestling with his father, what do you mean?" He responded: "What I mean? I mean they were rolling around on the floor and he had his old man by the balls!"

The court reporter, a pretty young thing, blanched; my son almost fell out of his chair, and on the way home, he told me he did not think he would become a lawyer.

John Blackwell
New Iberia

I participated in a unique deposition south of Galveston, Texas, many years ago. It involved a maritime case and a key witness who was about to go offshore as a diver. The deposition was scheduled at the last minute and lawyers had traveled from New Orleans and Houston to the diver's home. When we arrived at the deponent's home, his wife sent us out back where he was practicing dives in his own tank. We all gathered around the tank (with the court reporter present) and began asking questions. Every 10 minutes or so, the diver would put his on helmet and go underwater for a few minutes, come back up, remove his helmet and answer a few more questions. The whole deposition took approximately two hours to complete, at least half of which time was occupied by the lawyers sitting around the tank waiting for the witness to return from underwater. Once we got used to the scenario, it was actually an enjoyable experience.

Larry Roedel
Baton Rouge

In the late 1970s I was involved in a wrongful death case. One of the witnesses could not give her deposition until after 6:00 p.m. because of her work schedule and because she was a student at LSU (she was 21 years old and most of us were in our 20's or 30's). The lawyers agreed to accommodate her and met one evening after hours. She arrived at the appointed time; she was a true beauty and was extremely pleasant during the deposition.

Although we thought she had some liability, most

of the attorneys (all were male) did not "grill" her. After the deposition, all of the lawyers discussed the case, but most were still thinking about the young lady.

A few days later, I was looking for my file on the case and could not find it. After searching our office, I called the law firm where the deposition had been taken, and they said they would look for it. Later that afternoon I got a call from the opposing counsel, who told me they had found my file and it was at the front desk. I immediately went to their office, which was only a few blocks away, and picked up the file.

When I picked up the file, I noticed it had a perfume smell and something pink was sticking out of the side. I walked outside to where my car was parked in front of their office, put the file on top of my car, and pulled a pink envelope from my file. It was addressed to me.

Inside was a perfumed, handwritten letter in a woman's handwriting which began, "Dearest Jack," and went on to say how much the young lady had enjoyed my taking her deposition and that she wanted to see me again. It was signed, "Your Love Slave."

I was in total shock for a brief moment, thinking the letter was for real. Then I turned around and saw every member of the law firm and their support staff with their noses pressed upon every window of their office in complete hysterics.

Jack Dampf
Baton Rouge

CHAPTER VIII

THE JURY

1. A Jury of One's Peers?

One common quip is that a jury is composed of 12 people who were not smart enough to avoid jury duty. Some of the following stories tend to support that premise. The first, and easily one of the best, comes from Judge Eugene Davis of New Iberia.

> I am a great believer in the jury system but the following story is a good response to one who waxes overly long about the collective intelligence and wisdom of the jury.

> In the early 1980s, I set out to review and edit my form jury instructions and special verdict forms to take out the legalisms and make the forms "gender neutral." One change I made on my special verdict form was to substitute "foreperson" for "foreman" just above the signature line at the bottom of the final page. In the very first trial in which I used this new verdict form, the jury reached a verdict, and the bailiff handed the verdict form to me. I read the answers to the questions and they made perfect sense. My eyes then fell on the signature line. Four of the six jurors had squeezed their signatures on the signature line just above my gender neutral "foreperson".

Here is another contribution:

> A hotly contested wrongful death case was about to begin in Pointe Coupee Parish. Plaintiff's counsel, anxious to weed out potential adverse jurors, closely questioned each member of the venire about his or her work, hobbies, philosophy, and other relevant matters. One prospective juror was a middle-aged gentleman of modest means who worked as a short order cook. The prospective juror listened carefully and gave short, direct answers to each question. It seemed clear that the lawyer didn't

particularly want this particular person on the jury, but could find no grounds to challenge him for cause. Finally he asked:

Q: Mr. _____, you know we only want fair-minded people on this jury, don't you?

A: Yes.

Q: It wouldn't be right to have someone sit who couldn't be fair, would it?

A: No.

Q: Well, is it possible that you might harbor some subconscious bias against my client?

A: How would I know?

The prospective juror, who obviously was a very careful listener, was challenged nonetheless, but not for cause.

C. G. "Woody" Norwood
New Orleans

At the conclusion of a first day of a jury trial, the Court instructed the jurors to return to their same seats the next day at 9:00 a.m. On the second day, juror #2 was missing from the second seat, and the judge asked the marshal to make the appropriate phone calls to determine his whereabouts. Shortly thereafter the marshal informed the judge that the juror had left his house early that morning with the intention of returning to court. The judge instructed the marshal to search the courthouse to see if the juror could be found. About an hour later, the marshal approached the bench and informed the judge of his progress, and we lawyers noticed a smile on the judge's face. He called us up to the bench and told us that we may not want this particular juror on the panel. It appears that the marshal had found him sitting alone in the second seat in the jury box in the third floor empty courtroom, directly below the vacant second seat in our courtroom on the fourth floor. Without further ado, counsel agreed to moving in an alternate juror.

Bob Young
New Orleans

Smitty Landry of New Iberia submits this observation of the "peer" jury.

Many years ago I was associated with a wizened, street-smart New Orleans lawyer in the representation of a plaintiff in a personal injury case in federal court in the Crescent City. The case was being tried in Judge Christenberry's court before a 12 person jury. At that time the federal district courtrooms were located in the old Department of Wildlife and Fisheries building on Royal Street. The building, now beautifully renovated to house the Louisiana Supreme Court, is situated on an entire block between Royal and Chartres Streets.

At that time, I was new to the practice, and working with this lawyer was an eye-opener, to say the least. In his witness preparation, for instance, when he asked the plaintiff what answer he would give to a particular question on cross-examination, and the witness replied in a manner not to the lawyer's liking, the lawyer would say: "No, that's not what you're going to say. This is what you are going to say," and to my amazed consternation would proceed to tell him what to say in answer to the question.

After the usual formalities, we picked the jury, which could be fairly, if sadly, described as forlorn and bedraggled. My senior associate counsel was ecstatic because he believed that the least intelligent, least sophisticated jury would be most favorable to our client's cause. He described the jury's limitations, which he liked very much, in this manner:

"You see that jury? You could take every one of them and head them out of the front door on Royal Street, and there's not a one of them who could find his way to Arnaud's."

2.   Voir Dire

During jury selection in New Roads, Judge Jack Marionneaux had filled the jury box with members of the venire and was asking a series of general questions to determine whether they were qualified to serve as jurors. One of the questions was whether the prospective juror could read and write. Apparently not wanting to be embarrassed, one juror told Judge Marionneaux that he could read and write. When he did so his wife, who was seated in the back of the courtroom, jumped up and started hollering at him to quit lying to the judge. As she proceeded toward the jury box, she told the court that her husband could neither read nor write. Before Judge Marionneaux could react, she reached the jury box, grabbed the gentleman by his ear and started pulling him out, telling the court that he was not qualified to be a juror and that she was taking him home where he could "do some work around the house." All of the lawyers and Judge Marionneaux sat somewhat dumbfounded as the pair left the courtroom.

Mike Pulaski
New Orleans

The defendant was on trial for a serious felony, and all day long prospective jurors had been asked about their fairness. The defense attorney explained over and over that an ideal juror, to be fair, waits until all the evidence has been presented, including the defendant's evidence and argument, before making a decision about guilt or innocence.

Then each prospective juror was asked if he or she

could be such an ideal juror. The final question was "if you were sitting in the defendant's place, what kind of juror would you like to have judge you?" All day long the responses from prospective jurors were "one that can be fair" or "one that will not decide the case until all the evidence has been presented" or "one that will wait to hear my side of the case."

One older prospective juror had been listening to the responses all day long, but when asked what type of juror he would like to have sitting on his case if he were the defendant, stated: "I would like to have a person that came into the courtroom and took one look at me and decided that I was innocent, and never changed his mind no matter what the evidence was against me."

Justice Jeff Victory
Shreveport

Jury selection had proceeded all day in a serious criminal case. Each prospective juror was grilled about the presumption of innocence, and was told that if at that time one was required to vote on guilt or innocence, one would have to vote "not guilty" because no evidence had yet been presented. Finally, each juror was asked if he had formed an opinion at that stage of the trial as to the defendant's guilt.

When the last prospective juror of the day, who had been witnessing this repetitive voir dire all day long, was asked if he had formed an opinion as to the defendant's guilt, he replied: "Well, no, I haven't. But somebody around here thinks he did something wrong, because he's the one sitting over there in the defendant's chair. It's not me and it's not you and I know they didn't draw his name out of a hat."

Justice Jeff Victory
Shreveport

A defendant who was charged with burglary was represented by a young lawyer who had recently been admitted to the bar and who was abounding in the knowledge of the many rights protecting an accused. He apparently had recently heard or read of the often recited cliché that an accused enters the courtroom under a cloak of innocence and must be acquitted unless the state proves his guilt beyond a reasonable doubt. During voir dire of a somewhat elderly woman who barely met the literacy requirements to serve as a juror, and who was very unhappy to have been summoned for jury duty, the young attorney, dressed in his finest suit, a new white oxford shirt with buttoned-down collar and a very conservative striped tie, looked seriously into the eyes of the prospective juror and in his best diction and most resonant voice, loud enough for all prospective jurors and a filled courtroom to hear, asked: "Mrs. Williams, I read you the law about the presumption of innocence in Louisiana and in the entire United States. Do you look upon my client, who has just entered this courtroom and who is seated at this table, as an innocent man?" After a long and careful look at the accused, she replied: "He don't look so innocent to me." Everyone in the courtroom burst into laughter. The lawyer had no further questions. He returned to his chair and sat down, knowing he had just spent his first peremptory challenge. I don't think he ever asked that question again.

Judge Harold Brouillette
Marksville

Called to jury duty was a gentleman from north Louisiana who in his younger days was well known as one prone to drinking excessively, to fighting, and to generally "raising hell." In his later years, he had become a church-going, upstanding member of the community, although he still possessed some of his temper. He came to jury duty wearing his brand new western suit and string tie and his white Stetson cowboy hat, which he proceeded to place in his lap upon taking the voir dire stand. After the district attorney had finished voir dire, the defense attorney began his questioning. He informed the gentleman that there would be law enforcement officers testifying, and pointed out that their testimony should not be entitled to any more belief than the testimony of any one else. The prospective juror responded that he wasn't sure about that. The defense attorney became indignant and told the juror that just because a person wore a uniform, he or she wasn't more worthy of belief than anyone else. The juror replied again, as calm as he could, that he wasn't certain of that. After several more questions along this line, the defense attorney became more and more indignant and, moving closer to the juror, said "surely you don't mean that just because a deputy sheriff gets up here and tells us something, that we're supposed to believe him?" The prospective juror replied: "God damn it mister, the only thing I can tell you, is every time they brought me up here, I had done exactly what they said I did." The defense attorney had no more questions.

Justice Chet Traylor
Winnsboro

When I came to the bench, the accused already had been tried before a six-person jury which had failed to reach a decision. The district attorney decided to try him again. Unable to post bond, the accused had been in prison for six months on a charge of Aggravated Burglary. The victim, 74 years of age, was now in a nursing home in a different parish, and the trial was held in a small auditorium of that nursing home. This was my first trial as a judge.

The judge's "bench" was a chair, the witness chair was to my right, fronting mine a couple of feet or so. The space in front of us stayed open, but on either side, facing each other, were the jury chairs to the front and a bit right of the witness chair, and the District Attorney's chair to my left front, the Defendant attorney's chair beside it, and the defendant's chair last.

Important to understanding the humor involved is this occurrence at jury selection. Prior to jury selection, a young Afro-American, tall and lanky, approached the bench and offered, as an excuse to be relieved of jury duty, "heavy watery" eyes. He did not have a doctor's certificate and I refused his request. He was obviously unhappy with my decision. Prior to being summoned for jury duty, he had spent his life on a farm; he was not comfortable with the "sophistication" of the "big city" (population 3,000) and courtrooms. Unhappily for him, he was one of the jurors chosen.

Unfortunate also was his seating at the trial: in the first juror's seat, which was the chair nearest to and almost in front of the witness chair. The trial began and he lounged in his chair, long legs protruding out into the aisle; his hands were tucked under his chin, and his eyes stood at half-mast. He was pointedly disinterested. He was sulking. He did not want to be there.

The D.A. called the gray-haired, elderly victim as his first witness. The victim's answers had the D.A. in smiles. To every question that permitted it, the victim replied: "he hit me in the jaw! He knocked me to the floor! He kicked me in the ribs and stole my case of Coca-Colas. I'll never forget that face!"

Having successfully established that the victim had suffered this "heinous" (D.A.'s classification) crime, the D.A. confidently posed two crucial questions:

"Sir, is the man who committed this crime in the courtroom today?"

"Yes, he is. He hit me in the jaw! He knocked me to the floor! He kicked me in the ribs and stole my case of

Coca-Colas! I'll never forget that face!"

The D.A.'s smile almost became a smirk as he asked:

"Sir, will you point him out for the jury?"

Recall that the lanky juror was lounging in the juror's chair next to me, long legs protruded into the aisle. His eyes were at "half-mast," and he was pointedly disinterested and sulking. He was right next to the witness.

"Yes, sir," the victim exclaimed vehemently! At this point he leaned forward and pointed his long finger right in the lanky juror's face, almost touching his nose, and nearly screamed: "I'll never forget that face! He hit me in the jaw! He knocked me down! He kicked me in the ribs and stole my case of Coca-Colas!"

The juror's eyes popped open. For several seconds his eyes were riveted on the tip of the accusing finger, only inches away from his nose. Then he tried to smile, turning his head to look at the other jurors. But all eyes and attention were now focused on him! His smile was so contrived that, on trial for any crime, he would have been convicted. He was frightened to the point of near panic.

What he was thinking appeared crystal clear to me: "I didn't want to be here in the first place and now this crazy old man is going to put me in jail. Sure as I'm sitting here, I'm going to jail and I never wanted to be here in the first place. I'm going to jail and there isn't anyone who can help me!" Stark fear was written on all his features.

Switch now to the D.A., whose smile has disappeared. His face and bald head match each other; both are bright beet-red. An uncomfortable quiet settles on the courtroom. The D.A. tries to collect himself and finally stutters unintelligibly. In the interim the victim, realizing that something is amiss, looks about for the first time, sees the defendant sitting in the last chair on his left and blurts out: "You've tried to fool me. You were hiding him from me. There he is over there," pointing now at the defendant.

Needless to say, I granted a mistrial.

Judge Paul Newell
Minden

Another reason why persons seek to avoid jury duty is reflected in this story provided by Judge Eugene Davis of New Iberia:

A member of the jury venire tried a new excuse each week for a month to get excused from jury duty for an upcoming civil docket. When he did not show up for duty on the assigned date, I directed the bailiff to arrest him and bring him to court. I had completed jury selection when the bailiff arrived with the wayward juror. My prospective juror's explanation that he had forgotten his summons did not ring true, in light of his repeated requests to be excused from service. After a brief hearing in the presence of the jury, I held the wayward juror in contempt for deliberately refusing to comply with the jury summons. I devised what I thought was a fair, imaginative sentence: 24 hours in the parish jail, suspended on condition that during the week long trial which was underway, he would sit on the front row behind the rail in the courtroom and keep the same hours the trial jury kept. As I was preparing to go on the bench after the noon break on the second day of trial, the bailiff came in and said, "Judge, your juror said to tell you that he will just serve his sentence." I signed a commitment order and never saw the prospective juror again. (Actually, I signed two orders, one committing him for 24 hours and another releasing him after four hours.) When we resumed our civil trial, I called the attorneys to the bench for a conference and told them they needed to liven up the trial a bit; their only spectator had elected to go to jail rather than suffer through the rest of the trial.

Attempting to avoid jury duty has become something of a national pastime. One female judge won the game by an appeal to national patriotism. Looking at a line of about 30 people who stood up to request excuses from jury duty, she advised the group that she considered jury service to be one of the premier duties of American citizenship and that such service was of a sacrificial nature, just as responding to the call to serve in the Armed Forces. She then told them she would consider their requests for excuses but they would be granted only if they were very serious because "when my husband left for Vietnam in August 1967, I can assure you he was not given the opportunity to call a judge and ask to be excused because it was not convenient for him to go that day." All but two of the 30 prospective jurors immediately sat down.

One prospective juror's belief that he was exempt from jury duty triggered an unusual chain of events. A state legislator was served a jury summons in Vermilion parish, but believing he was exempt, failed to appear at trial. The judge issued a bench warrant and when the legislator was brought in, he was adjudged in contempt of court and fined. Thereafter he was selected as a juror, and subsequently elected foreman of the jury. The case was a first degree murder case in which the defendant shot the victim in a crowded bar. His plea was self defense. The court usually reconvened at 1:30 p.m. after the lunch break; however, on the third morning, the judge, eager to complete the trial that day, announced at the noon break that court would reconvene at 1 p.m. Defense counsel, engrossed in his work, failed to hear or comprehend the change. Thus when defense counsel strolled back into court at 1:20 p.m., the irate judge found him in contempt and levied a fine. Later that evening the case went to the jury, which bought the self defense plea and exonerated the defendant. This strange turn of events prompted one wag to comment: "That's an example of justice in Louisiana; a man shoots another in front of 50 people and goes Scot free, but his defense lawyer and the foreman of the jury end up paying fines."

3. Jury Misconduct

The lawbooks contain many cases in which jurors, during the course of a trial, have improper contact with the parties or their attorneys, or otherwise disregard the judge's instructions. Here are some instances of juror "misconduct" that didn't make the lawbooks:

> I was defending a personal injury suit in a jury trial before Judge Isom Guillory, Jr., in St. Landry Parish. As my medical expert was being cross-examined and in what I perceived to be the crucial part of the examination, an elderly gentleman suddenly rose out of his seat in the back row of the jury box and nonchalantly strode out of the box and onto the courtroom floor. He had reached about halfway across the room when Judge Guillory noticed him. Staring in disbelief, Judge Guillory brought the man to an abrupt halt with a sharp rap of his gavel and the acidic query "What are you doing?!" Sounding as though the judge would surely understand, the elderly gentleman responded, "Judge, its four o'clock and my ride home gets here at four o'clock so I'm going home." Another sharp rap of Judge Guillory's gavel and his somewhat scathing directive to "get back in there!" sent the juror scurrying back into the box with a great deal less aplomb than he had shown in leaving it.

> Jimmy Dauzat
> Opelousas

> The late Judge William Fleniken observed a man crossing the courtroom floor inside the rail separating the spectator section from the counsel tables, jury box and bench. The judge ordered the man to sit down next to the defense attorney. The man protested but the judge was insistent. Finally, the bailiff approached the bench and told the judge that the man was not a defendant but a juror and was trying to get to the jury box.

> Judge James E. Clark
> Shreveport

One of my partners, who must go unnamed, was defending a Jones Act case in federal court in St. Louis, Missouri. As the jury filed out of the courtroom after rendering a defense verdict, one of the female jurors winked at my partner. The plaintiff's counsel, after observing this, demanded that the court recall the juror for questioning. The judge gently took the juror through a line of questioning designed to determine whether she had had any contact with my partner outside the courtroom. She advised the court that she had never met my partner, had never spoken to him, and, in fact, had never seen him outside the courtroom. Accordingly, the judge asked, "Well then, why did you wink at him as you walked out of the courtroom?" The juror replied, "Because I think he is cute." The judge turned to the plaintiff's counsel and said, "What can I do? He is cute."

Hal Welch
New Orleans

This story is apochyrphal, or the same event occurred in several states at about the same time. As the story goes, a five day jury trial was winding down. As the parties broke for lunch, it appeared that the evidence would close early in the afternoon and the case would go to the jury that day. When the court reconvened after lunch, the judge called both counsel to the bench and asked them to casually observe juror no. 6 and tell him if she looked like the same woman who had been sitting in that jury seat during the first four and a half days of trial. Each did so and whispered to the judge that she definitely was not the same person. The judge, reading from his jury chart, asked Mrs. X to stand. No one did. The judge then directed his comment to the woman in seat no. 6, and asked, "You are not Mrs. X, are you?" "No," came the reply, "she's my sister-in-law, and she has a hairdresser appointment this afternoon and she asked me to sit in for her a couple of hours."

Every trial lawyer knows the danger of asking the question on voir dire which can turn the jurors and prospective jurors against the questioner and his client. One probably apocryphal tale is about the lawyer who asked the middle aged woman whether she or anyone in her family had any serious involvement with the criminal law. When she made an affirmative response, the lawyer asked her to tell about the family member and the crime. Her response was that she'd prefer not to talk about it. When the voir-diring lawyer asked the same question again, the juror asked the judge if she was required to elaborate, and he told her she was. The lawyer repeated the question, and her answer, told tearfully, was that when she and her family first arrived in that area from another state, her son had been charged with first degree murder and had been convicted and executed. After that, the voir-diring lawyer did not have a friend in the courthouse, perhaps not even his client.

Another example is this excerpt from the voir dire in a criminal case in federal court:

> THE COURT: Hi. Ms. _____ . If you'll sit down right there please.
>
> A: All right.
>
> THE COURT: You indicated that you had been a victim of a crime?
>
> A: No. I spent time in St. Gabriel Prison and I was later pardoned.
>
> THE COURT: And what were you charged with?
>
> A: Conspiracy.
>
>   * * *
>
> DEFENSE ATTORNEY: That experience with the judicial system, has that had any effect on you?
>
> A: Well, it was really a hurtful thing to be away from my child at that time. But it

made me understand. It made me understand a lot of things. And, it changed my opinion on a lot of things.

DEFENSE ATTORNEY: Like what?

A: Like people say: Oh, he got life in prison instead of the death penalty; the victim is dead. Well, I can tell you from the life of the people that were sentenced to live in prison. They would have preferred to be executed.

DEFENSE ATTORNEY: Okay.

A: And it was a hard thing. Because even in the middle of the night, in that prison, you would hear them in the night; and you've never heard such despair and shame and crying. To never have anything except being treated like an animal.

THE COURT: Any further questions? (No response.)

CHAPTER IX

DEMONSTRATIONS

Out of court demonstrations (tests and experiments) are the stuff of which expert testimony is made. In court demonstrations are rare, partly because they are too expensive and time consuming, and partly because a "backfiring" demonstration can turn a winning case into a loser. The classic is the "Count's" discharge of a firearm in court; probably few lawyers over 50 today did not hear that story in their early years of practice. Several versions of the Count's failed demo were sent to us; the one below came from Homer Ed Barousse, who practices in the Count's hometown of Crowley. Several other attorneys sent in courtroom demo stories which are reproduced below:

1. "Count Carmouche and the Misfiring Revolver"

Emile "Count" Carmouche was a local legend as a criminal defense lawyer. The Count practiced law in Crowley until his early 90s; only eight days elapsed between his last day at the office and his funeral. He was always sharp, but in his younger days, he was something to behold.

During the late 1940s, the Count was involved in a murder trial in which the prosecution identified the defendant's handgun as the murder weapon. The defendant admitted that the revolver belonged to him, but maintained that he never used it because it always misfired.

The Count privately interrogated his client in detail about the handgun's propensity to misfire and believed his client, so he decided to demonstrate to the jury that the revolver would not fire. He consulted with Judge Smith Hoffpauir, the trial court judge, and with the prosecutor, and the judge agreed that the Count could demonstrate to the jury that the revolver would not fire if he could do it safely.

The story goes that the jury, the prosecutor, Judge Hoffpauir, the Count, and the entire throng-of spectators went out to the front grounds[4] of the Acadia Parish Courthouse. The Count addressed the jury, informing them that the defendant's revolver could not be the murder weapon because it always misfired. Sheriff Walter Larcade loaded the revolver and handed it to the Count. The Count pointed the revolver in the air and said, "This will be the proof that you need to exonerate this innocent man." He then pulled the trigger. After the revolver fired, the Count turned to Judge Hoffpauir and said under his breath, "I just shot my client into the goddamned electric chair."

2.   **"The Dog that Didn't Hunt, but Sicced"**

Some years ago, a noted criminal defense lawyer from St. Landry Parish was defending a man on a charge of manslaughter in a trial before Judge Isom Guillory, Jr., in Opelousas. The defendant's German Shepherd, "Fido," allegedly had attacked the victim at the command of the defendant, inducing the victim's fatal heart attack. As part of his defense that the attack had not occurred, the lawyer was attempting to show the gentle nature of "Fido." As a demonstration, he urged Fido to "sic" his co-counsel. Fido casually walked over to the co-counsel, gently laid his head in his lap, and began to lick his hand. Emboldened by this success and eager to convince the judge that this was not something contrived, the attorney added "This will work on anyone." He then pointed to the courtroom bailiff, and commanded Fido to "sic him!" The bailiff, who bore an uncanny resemblance to Barney Fife of the old

---

[4] One version of the story is that the demonstration took place in the courtroom, with a resulting collapse of the ceiling upon the jury.

"Mayberry RFD" TV series, had been peacefully dozing in a chair, leaning back against the courtroom wall about 20 feet from the counsel table. At the instant of the command, Fido's ears flattened against his head and his lips curled into a vicious snarl, revealing a set of huge white fangs. With a deep-seated growl, Fido lunged across the counsel table and headed for the bailiff, who had by this time sufficiently aroused himself to understand his position of imminent peril; his attempt to escape sent him sprawling backwards, arms and legs flailing in the air. Fortunately, the co-counsel had a hand on Fido's leash and prevented the dog from executing his colleague's directive. The judge furiously hammered his gavel and thundered, "Restrain the animal!" at the properly chastened defense attorney. Order eventually was restored to the courtroom. The bailiff escaped generally unscathed, no doubt wondering why he had been arbitrarily selected for this show of supposed canine geniality. The attorney's client was not so fortunate.

Jimmy Dauzat
Opelousas

3. The Edwards Brothers

In his younger days, former Governor Edwin Edwards was renowned as a brilliant trial attorney. During the mid-1950s, Edwin was honing his skills as a criminal defense attorney. His brother, Nolan, was practicing with him, and in their younger days, they looked remarkably alike. They were the same height and build, and had the same appearance, with dark hair turning gray.

After he examined the prosecution's key witness in one of his criminal defenses, Edwin realized he had problems with the witness. He concluded that his only hope of acquittal was to prove that the witness did not properly identify the defendant. Everything was riding on Edwin's ability to discredit the eyewitness.

The cross examination was interrupted by the noon break. Over the noon hour, Edwin and Nolan decided upon a risky but dramatic strategy. They switched clothes and returned to court in their exchanged wardrobes, and Nolan continued the cross examination, with Edwin sitting next to him and wearing the clothing that Nolan had worn that morning.

Nolan asked all of the necessary prerequisite questions to again challenge the witness' memory, and finally extracted a statement from the witness that he was "positive" in his identification of the defendant. Nolan then asked the magic question. "Do you remember me cross-examining you earlier during the day before the noon hour?" The witness retorted without hesitation, "No, but I remember your brother was wearing that suit that you are wearing and he cross-examined me before noon." A plea bargain was confected within the hour.

Homer Ed Barousse
Crowley

4.   Sometimes Things Work Out Right

During the course of a trial which lasted over five weeks, we introduced into evidence a vial of carbon black, a substance, emitted by the defendant's plant, which our clients contended was getting all over their houses and clothes, and in their nostrils. Late one afternoon during the trial, Judge Hunter asked his bailiff to hand him the vial of carbon black. While the testimony and the presentation of evidence continued, I could see Judge Hunter opening the vial and sprinkling some carbon black in front of him, presumably on a piece of paper. Shortly thereafter, Judge Hunter was seen shaking what apparently was the piece of paper into a waste basket. Shortly after that, the bailiff and the lawyers in the courtroom noticed that there were black smudges and smears on Judge Hunter's face. The bailiff called this to the attention of the judge, who looked down and saw that his hands were also black. As Judge Hunter was removing his glasses with his wrists, he recessed the trial for the remainder of the day.

I began loading my brief case and laughing to myself that this had been a very good day indeed. Before any of the lawyers left the courtroom, the bailiff rushed in from Judge Hunter's office asking all of the lawyers to come to the judge's office. The bailiff guided us through the door behind the bench, usually used only by the judge and his staff. As we reached the judge's office, the judge, standing behind his desk, pointed to the floor and said in a loud voice, "Look at that, look at that!!" On Judge Hunter's luxurious carpet, all the way from the entrance to his office to his desk, were distinct black footprints.

A great day of trial had gotten even better.

John B. (Spike) Scofield
Lake Charles

5.   A Word From A Sponsor?

Many years ago, I was in a jury trial in Napoleonville before Judge Adolphe Menuet. There were several defendants, and the case involved determining who was responsible for a fire that destroyed an expensive mobile home that had been brought in for the installation of a pop-up vent on its roof. One of the issues was whether the radio, which had been installed by one of the co-defendants, had "shorted out," causing the fire. One of the lawyers had hired an expert to demonstrate at trial that the radio worked perfectly and therefore it could not have been the cause of the fire. To demonstrate at trial, the expert hooked up the radio to two large speakers placed in front of a hushed jury. He then turned on the radio at full volume, and the first thing that everyone heard was a commercial asking the booming question, "Are you suffering from hemorrhoids?" The jury cracked up.

O'Neal Walsh
Baton Rouge

CHAPTER X

CRIMINAL CASES

1. Clothes Make the Man?

Judge James E. Clark of Shreveport provides this classic tale:

> I was presiding in criminal court on a day when we took care of a variety of cases, including guilty pleas. A name was called and a man came forward, accompanied by his lawyer. The man was dressed in a tuxedo, a blue ruffled tux shirt and patent leather black shoes. His attorney asked to approach the bench with the D.A., and said quietly that he wanted to discuss his client's attire. My immediate response was "Please do so."
>
> He said his client was there to plead guilty on a plea bargain worked out with the D.A. The client had asked his lawyer what he should wear to court, and the lawyer told him that it was a pretty formal occasion and that he should dress appropriately. That morning the client arrived dressed in the tux, telling the lawyer that he had rented the tux and all that went with it for $45.00, which was all the money he had.
>
> As this was being related, I lowered my head and put my hand to cover my face: I dared not laugh, with the man standing there seeing us talking but not hearing us. The attorney asked me to not hold it against his client, who was not trying to put us down but was trying to show respect. My response was that if this was a con job, it was one of the best ever pulled on me. I suspended the fine and court costs and sent him away on probation.

Tom Davenport of Monroe provides these illustrations of how clothes can unmake the man:

> During a preliminary examination in state court,

the sales clerk of a victimized western clothing store testified how two men had used a stolen Visa credit card to purchase various items of clothing. One of the men presented the stolen card to pay for purchases made by both of the men. The clerk could not identify my client as being either of the two men making purchases charged to the Visa card. However, the clerk did recall, with particularly, several of the items purchased and charged to the stolen credit card. One purchase he described was a pair of burnt orange full quill ostrich cowboy boots. When the clerk's description was complete, I heard a shuffling sound beneath the counsel table beside me where my client was seated. I carefully and casually glanced under the table and yes – my client was wearing a pair of burnt orange full quill ostrich cowboy boots which suddenly had become too warm for his comfort.

During the first day of a multiple count drug distribution trial, the undercover agent testified about his telephone contacts with a drug dealer arranging the transactions which later occurred and which were the basis of the charges against my client. Fortunately, the undercover agent had never met my client and knew the party with whom he was making arrangements only by the name "PECK". On the second day of trial my client arrived late, entered the courtroom with the jury seated and waiting, and was admonished by the judge to remove his visor in the courtroom. He removed his custom made leather visor, on the brim of which was imprinted "PECK".

2.   A Man Who is his Own Lawyer Has....

Sam D'Amico of Baton Rouge provides this story of a criminal defendant who perhaps was too smart to be a lawyer:

Several years ago a young man charged with burglary and theft had been sent to the mental hospital at Jackson. While there, he was injured in an attempt to escape, and was sent to Charity Hospital in New Orleans for treatment. While in the hospital, he managed to leave his room and find a telephone. He called Western Union and, representing himself to be the Sheriff of East Baton Rouge Parish, had a telegram sent to the Charity Hospital in New Orleans authorizing his release. He was released. Thereafter, he appeared at my office requesting that I seek to determine if there was any outstanding arrest warrant for him. Immediately following my call to the sheriff's office confirming there was an arrest warrant, two deputies arrived and escorted him to the parish prison.

One of Sam's defendants in an arson case arrived early on the second morning of the trial and placed flowers and cigars on the seats of the jurors. The result: a hung jury!

3. Pleas, Please

Anyone who has sat in criminal court at a plea session knows the darndest things can occur. Once a defendant who had been in jail for about three months pleaded guilty to a reduced misdemeanor drug offense and was given a time-served sentence. When he apparently did not understand the sentence, the judge told him that he had nothing more to do and could go home after he gave the Sheriff back his prison jumpsuit. He looked at the judge and said, "that's no problem," unzipped the jumpsuit, and started undressing.

On another occasion the judge was taking the guilty plea of a man charged with first offense driving while intoxicated. When the judge asked the defendant what his social security number was, he could not remember it so he reached in his pocket to get his wallet. When he started to pull out the wallet, a small plastic bag filled with vegetable-like material fell out onto the courtroom floor. The man looked at the package, "wet himself," and fainted.

When I was new on the bench, a young man was before me charged with theft of about $20 worth of gasoline through the use of another person's credit card. He immediately pled guilty and said he did it because he was penniless and that he had a wife and child and just didn't feel he had a choice. Upon hearing that impassioned plea, I was overcome with sorrow and was about to reach into my pocket for money to help him out. The assistant D.A. stopped me with his comment: "Judge, please don't sentence this man right now. He is wanted on warrants out of Florida for a large number of thefts, and we want to get that information to you before sentencing." I was not quite as compassionate with him after receiving that information.

Judge James E. Clark
Shreveport

During the trial of a simple battery charge in Monroe City Court, the "tangle-tongued" client was asked under direct examination about prior criminal convictions. His response simply was: "None other than driving a drunk car."

Before ruling on cases, a judge has to learn new words, not the array of Latin and French words and their Americanized mispronounciations which are part of the usual law school training, but words used by parties or witnesses. For example, in a spousal support case, the young wife does not need a "car"; she needs a "way to go." A criminal defendant, trying to represent himself, comes to court for his "arrangement" and asks for a "change of vengeance" because he wants his trial moved to a different parish. He may not like the prosecutor, Mr. Hatchet (whose real name is really Hatch), or he many have some doubts about his indigent defender, Jim Beal, who has also presided as magistrate in mayor's court and is known to him as "Judge Jim Beam."

A criminal defendant was charged with second degree murder in the Twenty Second Judicial district court. Shortly before his trial was scheduled to begin, he filed a pro se motion to discharge his attorney and enroll as counsel of record to represent himself. In support of his motion, he argued that he wanted someone who would represent him "jealously". He felt that his public defender was overburdened and would not "jealously" represent him. I denied his motion in part, but allowed him to enroll as "co-counsel" with his attorney.

After the defendant was convicted as charged by the jury, my court personnel and I bantered privately that he had apparently not represented himself "jealously" enough. We have also never let our public defender forget this incident, and occasionally question him as to whether he is representing his client "jealously".

Judge Donald M. Fendalson
Covington

After he was adjudged in contempt for non-payment of child support and was ordered to return to court to prove payment and purging of contempt, a rather large ex-professional football player confessed to me that he had not made the payments. I found him in contempt but informed him that as a favor I would allow him to serve his sentence on weekends so as to save his weekday job. He then told me that the child in question was born to his girlfriend, and that his wife was unaware of the situation. Then he asked a favor: "on those papers that show why I'm going to jail – can you say it was for fighting and drinking – cause my wife knows I do a little fighting and drinking?"

Judge Tony Graphia
Baton Rouge

It was arraignment day and the courtroom was full. Seated in the jury box were the inmates awaiting their turn. The process was orderly and uneventful until the bailiff called the name of one of the inmates and this elderly, unkept gentleman shuffled toward the bench. Despite his years, his raspy voice was strong and, when picked up by the podium microphone, boomed out into the audience, catching everyone's attention. "Yessir, I'm here!"

The assistant district attorney asked to approach

the bench and explained that the gentleman was homeless and apparently not completely in charge of his mental faculties. He had drifted into town and entered into a local business establishment, where he created a minor disturbance over some imagined wrong. He had been kept in jail overnight for his own good. The D.A. agreed to nolle prosse the charge if I would find out where the old man needed to go, and the Sheriff's office would provide transportation. So, this colloquy began:

> Q: (by the court)Sir, the D.A. is going to dismiss the charges against you. Do you have any business to keep you here in town?
>
> A: What you mean by "business"?
>
> Q: Do you have any connection to Cameron?
>
> A: Judge, I don't follow you.
>
> Q: I'm talking family. Do you have any children around here?
>
> (With that the old man smiled widely, stood tall and announced his answer to the world.)
>
> A: I just might, Judge – when I was young, I got around.
>
> The courtroom erupted into laughter. It seemed a good time for a recess.

Judge Ward Fontenot
Cameron

Judge Graydon Kitchens of Minden received the following letter from a prisoner who was awaiting sentencing:

> I am to be sentenced before you sir on are about the 3/2/87, Sir I like to imposes upon a little of your time if I may. Sir, I didn't commit this crime that I have been convicted of nor did I cosign it, but I omitt that I am a

principal in the crime, I am not the type to go into a person home and commit a crime. I have went into business and committed crimes and I can't say I want do it again, honestly, but its not my way to go into someone house and steal there belongings. I never ever done that. Sir, I am a thief but one with standards, A house, car, hotels, that's not what I do, now a warehouse, store, trains that's me. But I have back up from that since my discharge from prison from my bust in 79. I been working ever since, I did my time and got out of prison. Sir I don't like prison and I had to make a choice, to steal and go back or to work and I chose work...

Sir, I had to write you with my record before you already. You probably don't believe me – that's alright I don't believe I am writing you telling you this either.

4. They Ain't Always the Swiftest

Criminal defense lawyers can be frustrated by the lack of comprehension of some of their clients. Here are a few frustrating examples:

A young man in a country parish was brought before the judge for stabbing an opponent. The judge, who knew the young man's family and sought to instill some shame into his activities, asked him at sentencing: "John, I've known you from birth. You come from a good family; your mother and father have worked hard to take care of you, and were proud of you. How could you come to stab _____ with a knife? "Because, your honor," the young man replied, "That's all I had."

Cliffe Laborde
Lafayette

Early one morning a very upset woman came to my office seeking help. She stated that her husband was in jail and asked that I help her get him released.

I inquired about the charges against her husband and was told that he was charged with discharging a firearm in the neighborhood. I asked for details of the incident, and she told me her husband was disabled and that as he was sitting on his front porch with gun in hand, he became unhappy with her and began firing at her. Every time she stuck her head out from behind a tree, he took a shot at her. He missed each time.

She explained that her husband was really a fine man and that she would appreciate it if I would assist her in getting him released. This was successfully done after we explained to the District Attorney that it was a family matter and that the wife did not want to bring any charges against her husband and that she wanted him home with her.

I thought that this concluded the matter, but two days later both the wife and the husband came to my office, and she explained that she had one more job for me to do. It seems that the sheriff had refused to give them their gun back, and she wanted me to retrieve the weapon from the Sheriff's office.

This concluded our visit, and I sent them on their way.

Iddo Pittman
Hammond

"Turk" (fictitious name, of course) was 16 years old and looked like he should be playing nose guard on someone's football team. A Houston branch of one of the well known California street gangs had sent a recruiter to Shreveport to recruit into the gang boys aged 10 or 11 to 16 or 17. One of their principle functions was to steal cars, and the primary target was a "cutdog," more commonly known as an Oldsmobile Cutlass from 1988 to 1992. My client could have starred in the movie "Gone in

60 Seconds." Once he entered a car, he could start it and be gone in 30 seconds. Sometimes the gang would take three or four cars each night, after which they would take the cars to a rural area, take off the part (i.e. fender, door, etc.) that they were after, and then burn the car.

I met him when I was appointed to represent him after he and three or four of his fellow gang members were arrested trying to take their third or fourth car of that particular night. After stealing one car that later became stuck in the mud, they were foiled in their effort to steal another when the owner came upon the scene. My client was arrested about two blocks away.

When I first talked to him about the arrest and what had occurred, I asked him about statements he had given to the detectives who had arrested him. Because he was picked up two blocks away, it could be difficult for the district attorney to obtain a conviction without the statements. He told me that he had told the two detectives the whole story about the cars they had taken that night. The police had complete statements, but Turk contended that the statements "did not count." I asked him whether he had asked to see an attorney or whether they had called his guardian and he again said that he had talked to the detectives but the statements he gave them "did not count." I asked him why the statements "did not count," and he pointed to his legs, which were crossed one over the other in the usual manner that a person might sit, and said again that the statements "did not count".

This story may be more sad than humorous. I will never forget the look on his face as he told me that story, as he truly believed that those statements "did not count."

Eskridge Smith
Shreveport

A Vietnamese woman was scheduled to appear in court on a Wednesday morning. Her court-appointed lawyer had his secretary telephone her on Tuesday afternoon and give her directions to the courthouse. However, on Wednesday morning she failed to appear. About two hours later, her lawyer came to my office and reported that his client had called from the courthouse in Marshall, Texas. It seems that when his secretary gave her directions, she told her to come to the courthouse at Marshall and Texas. The defendant drove to the courthouse in Marshall, Texas. Fortunately, her lawyer had grown up in Marshall, and someone in the courthouse there knew he was a lawyer in Shreveport. I gave the lady a suspended sentence, believing she had suffered enough.

Judge James E. Clark
Shreveport

Towards the close of a two week federal mail and wire fraud trial my client insisted on testifying, against the strongest advice of counsel. The government contended a group of con men conspired with a Louisiana bank official to defraud gambling casinos in Las Vegas. Each of the group traveled to Las Vegas and registered in different casino hotels, none of which were linked to organized crime. They would then complete a credit application, giving a fictitious occupation or profession, which would refer the credit department to the colluding bank official for credit references and verification. This telephonic communication resulted in fraudulent credit information being given to the casino credit department and resulted in the applicant being extended the credit sought. At the end of the visit and after exhausting the line of credit, the guest would pay his gambling with a check on his account with the Louisiana bank. A stop payment order would then be entered on his check before it could be presented for payment on the account, which had only a nominal balance. After private protestation by counsel, my client took the stand to explain his innocence. On cross examination he was confronted with the credit application he had completed and was asked : "I see you stated in the credit application that you were a land developer – what land have you developed?" His response was: "I raked my yard once." Things thereafter went downhill rapidly.

Tom Davenport
Monroe

A story which was legend in Vermilion parish (and perhaps elsewhere) in the early fifties chronicled a criminal case of many years earlier, at a time at which electricity was not generally available and at which, at least in small towns, folks raised food in their backyards. One night such a homeowner shot a would-be thief in the homeowner's back yard, and was charged with assault and battery. After making bail, he contacted a local attorney and told him this story: shortly after dark, he heard chickens cackling in the rear of his house, so he lit a lantern, grabbed and loaded his shotgun, and opened the back door. As he did so, he caught the victim in the act of stealing some of his chickens. Then he told the attorney. "I yelled stop, thief, and he didn't stop but went to jump the fence with one of my chickens so I shot him in the ass." "Fine," said the attorney. "You have a good defense. We'll plead not guilty and I'll put you on the stand and I want you to tell the jury the story exactly as you've told it to me today, except don't say ass, say rectum." The trial came, the prosecution put on its witnesses, and the defendant took the stand. On prompting from his attorney, he began to tell his story, relating how he came to the back door with his shot gun. Then he continued: "I saw this fella there stealing my chickens, so I said stop, thief, and he went to jump over the fence, so I shot him in the .....I shot him in the... Lawyer, how do you call that fella's ass again?"

Smitty Landry of New Iberia sends in this story:

In a courtroom of the Sixteenth Judicial District Court in New Iberia, before Judge Ed Delahoussaye, appeared "Cool Breeze" Washington, a local non-violent police character, presenting himself for the umpteenth time on a charge of simple drunkenness.

In preparing to sentence him, Judge Delahoussaye asked the defendant if he had ever received treatment for his condition, and "Cool Breeze" replied: "Yes, judge, they sent me to Jackson, Louisiana."

"Well," continued the judge, "did they do anything for you there to help you?"

"Yeah, judge," answered "Cool Breeze," "they gave me some stuff to make me hate the taste of alcohol."

Asked by the judge if it helped him, "Cool Breeze" said "No, judge, I didn't take it."

"Why not?", countered the Judge.

With a serious expression and showing nothing but candor, "Cool Breeze" replied: "It interfered with my drinking."

Another story has it that two women were called to court after they fought over a man. When one of the women urged as her justification that she was "fighting for her man," the other woman told the judge that the gentleman in question wasn't her opponent's man, but a "much right" man. When the judge inquired what she meant, she responded, "one woman's got as much right to him as any other woman!"

5. Justice is a Sometimes Thing

Howard Gist of Alexandria sent us this story:

Judge Gaston Porterie appointed me to represent a man from Winnfield who was charged with bootlegging. Although they had found a still on the man's property, the federal agents did not do a very good job of making their case. The man convinced me that he was absolutely innocent of the charge. I put him on the stand and he gave a performance that would have earned him an Academy

Award. The jury let him go.

We met in the hall afterwards, where he thanked me and promised to send me a check in payment of my services (which he never did). Then he asked me if he could be prosecuted any further on that charge, and I told him that he was a free man. Thereupon he whispered in my ear "Well if you ever need any good corn whiskey, look me up."

John Lanier of Thibodaux relates this happening:

Like many young lawyers, I lost the first case I tried. Only a few days after having been sworn in, I was asked by my uncle, the senior partner in our firm, to defend a man who had been charged with shoplifting a bottle of whiskey. The defendant was a key employee of one of our regular clients, a well known sugar farmer.

The employee had been caught red-handed taking a bottle of whiskey from a small country store. Our client, the farmer, understood that his employee was guilty, but still needed his tractor driver for grinding season. He did not want him in jail.

The prosecutor was Elphage, our long time assistant D.A. The judge and Elphage had once been law partners, and the judge "read law" under Elphage to obtain his license to practice. (Until the second half of the twentieth century, one could "read law" while apprenticed to a licensed lawyer and, upon passing the bar exam, could be licensed even though he or she did not have a law degree from a university.) To say that the judge and Elphage were "tight" is an understatement.

During the course of the trial, Elphage sought to introduce the bottle which was allegedly taken by the defendant. It was just an ordinary whiskey bottle, a bottle of Old Crow. The only identification on the bottle was a price sticker which simply stated the price. It did not give the name of the store or have any other type of identification on it which would tie it to the store. Even the store owner couldn't swear that this particular bottle came from his store.

I objected to the introduction of the bottle as evidence, believing that I had a good objection. Elphage mumbled something about "substantial justice" in response to my objection. The judge overruled my objection, allowed the bottle into evidence, and convicted the tractor driver of shoplifting.

After the trial was over, Elphage told me, "Big John, you were right on your objection to that bottle. I know you were right, and the judge knows you were right. You know, however, that he took that bottle of whiskey. I know, and the judge knows it, too. Substantial justice has been done. Don't feel bad about it."

The defendant was sentenced to ten days in jail – to be served on weekends. That way he could continue working. Sometimes I think there is a lot to be said for "substantial justice."

6.   Rephrasing the Sentence

Sometimes a defendant will engage in self-help to avoid or mitigate punishment. Consider the defendant who was on trial for a serious crime for which he had posted bail. Each day he arrived at the trial nattily dressed, including expensive Italian leather loafers. On what probably would have been the last day of the trial, he arrived wearing tennis shoes. This fact did not escape the attention of the bailiff, who suspected foul play and alerted the sheriff's office. Sure enough, as the jury returned its verdict of "guilty," the defendant bolted for the door, making good time in his tennis shoes. Not good enough, however, for the two sheriff's deputies who were waiting for him right outside the door.

Here are some other examples:

Early in my career I represented a defendant in a federal crime prosecution who was charged with possession with intent to distribute 400 "bundles" of heroin. After his conviction by a jury, he was released on bond pending a pre-sentence investigation. On the date scheduled for his sentencing, he and his girlfriend arrived at my office several hours early. I met with him and discussed his prospects and then suggested he wait in the lobby until time to leave for court. We agreed to travel together to the courthouse, with the expectation that his girlfriend would drive me back to the office.

As the appointed time approached, I was taking a phone call in my office. Every few minutes my client would stick his head in the door, pointing to his watch. By the time I got off the phone, we were perilously tardy for court. We piled into the client's car, he driving, I in the front passenger seat, and his girlfriend in the rear. Typically, as we approached the U.S. Courthouse in the French Quarter there were no parking places to be had. We circled the block, but found each parking lot filled to capacity and the time for his court appearance passing. Finally, I spied a vacant spot and directed the client to pull in. "But, Mr. Murray," he observed, "there's a 'No Parking - Reserved for U.S. Marshals' sign."

"Ed," I responded, "you're about to be sentenced for 400 bundles of heroin. A parking ticket is the least of your worries. Park!"

He did and we rushed into the courthouse, ran up three flights of stairs, rushed into the courtroom and breathed a sigh of relief as we discovered the judge had not yet taken the bench. Later the crier called my client's case, and in response to Judge Jack Gordon's query about whether I had anything to say, I embarked upon the most eloquent plea of my yet young career. After acknowledging that my client was indeed charged and convicted of a most serious crime and confessing that yes, this was in fact his fourth conviction of a narcotics trafficking offense, I began to extol my personal belief in his many redeeming qualities. I concluded by asking for the court's mercy and requesting a sentence that would leave the defendant with the hope of returning to society within a reasonably anticipated lifetime.

After staring at me over the half glasses perched on the end of his nose, Judge Gordon responded: "I don't buy any of that, Mr. Murray. Your client is a career criminal. He has no respect for the law. You may think it a small thing, but as I returned from lunch a few minutes ago, I watched your client park in the Marshal's space."

Whereupon my client grabbed my arm and pleaded, "Tell him, Mr. Murray. Tell him!" Judge Gordon accepted my explanation and promised not to hold the parking incident against my client. Nevertheless, he imposed a sentence of forty years, without benefit of parole. I know in my heart that as my client enters into the last decade of his sentence, he is convinced that he is serving the next ten years for a parking violation.

Steve Murray
New Orleans

Some defendants want more punishment than the law is willing to give them. One example occurred in Caddo Parish in the late 1960s or early 1970s. A defendant plead guilty to spousal abuse; he allegedly struck his wife in an argument about vacation plans. When he was asked if he had done as charged, he responded in an obviously repentant voice: "Yes, sir, I'm not proud of it, but I did. Your Honor, may I try to explain?" When the court gave him permission to explain, he continued: "I had this two-week vacation coming and I was looking forward to going to some quiet place in the country, enjoying the sunshine, having three peaceful meals a day, talking with the fellows, no nagging at night, and being away from the wife and her family ..." and his voice trailed off. The court then ruled. "I find you guilty and sentence you to 14 days at CCI" [then the Parish lockup]. Do you know anything about CCI?" After getting a negative response, the court continued: "CCI is out in the country, you will have three reasonably good meals a day, have an opportunity to talk with the guys, have plenty of sunshine, and there will be no nagging for I will order that you not have any visitors." The judge then asked the prosecutor how long the defendant had been in jail prior to posting bond. When told it was three days, the judge added "And the 14 days will be subject to a credit of three days." With that, the defendant spoke up in a louder, more certain voice and said, "Your Honor, may I waive that credit?" "So ordered," said the court.

Some defendants have more time in criminal court than the average attorney. One repeater of non-violent offenses, designated as an outside security guard while serving a sentence, decided to escape but was readily recaptured He was then taken into court, and as his name was called he came forward with a measured step. Before anyone could say anything he intoned: "Your Honor, I waive counsel, waive arraignment, waive trial, plead guilty, waive judgment, and announce ready for sentencing. Judge, I just don't want to hear no more about it."

Finally, some defendants are not chastened by participation in a criminal proceeding. The old timers will remember that prior to World War II, the Mayor's Court was the place at which many small town misdemeanors were prosecuted. The mayor usually was not an attorney and there was no prosecutor; thus the procedure was remarkably informal. It was to such a mayor's court that the dispute between Alphonse and Etienne was referred. (Perhaps "dispute" is not the proper term: Alphonse became irritated at Etienne and knocked him down with one punch at a neighborhood bar, and Etienne, not much of a fighter, sought justification by filing a battery charge in mayor's court.) When the matter came for trial, the mayor inquired of the facts and learned that Alphonse had struck Etienne without any provocation or justification. He thus found Alphonse guilty and ordered him to pay a fine of $5. Hearing this, Alphonse asked incredulously: "You mean, it costs me $5 to hit Etienne?" When the mayor nodded affirmatively, Alphonse extracted a $10 bill from his wallet, handed it to the clerk, knocked Etienne down again, and strode out of court, satisfied with the bargain.

7.   Finding Humor in Every Situation

Before the days of the drug treatment programs, those who were found intoxicated were placed in jail to "dry out" and, after eight days, if they were not wanted for anything else, they were brought to court where the standard operating procedure was to give them eight days in jail, give them credit for time served, and turn them loose. We got to know them almost as friends. One day I told one regular, who we will call Sam, "I am tired of seeing you up here every Monday morning." He replied, "Judge, I can't help it if you can't get a promotion."

Judge Louis Doherty
Baton Rouge

I received many letters from inmates in jail and prison. One of my favorites began: "Dear Judge Clark, How are you? I am fine considering my environment."

Judge James E. Clark
Shreveport

8.   The "Birdshit" Defense

Tim McNamara of Lafayette relates this interesting story about how the phrase to identify a superficial defense was coined.

I learned a very important lesson as a rookie attorney in New Orleans sitting at the knee of the great master, P.A. (Prince Albert) Bienvenu, who first told me this story. It came about because I had heard the expression "that's a bird shit defense" made by various attorneys, and I inquired as to what it meant. I was then told this story. In the early 50s, there was a judge on the bench on the criminal district court by the name of Judge Bernard Cocke, a brilliant but irascible Irishman, highly respected by the bar because, although he had our profession's fondness for John Barleycorn, they believed he knew more criminal law drunk or sober than any other five judges in the State combined. One day there appeared before Judge Cocke a defendant accused of possession of marijuana who had pled not guilty to the charge and had decided to defend himself. Knowing something of the District Attorney's case, Judge Cocke strenuously urged the defendant should seek legal counsel before proceeding further, but the man was adamant, declaring that he knew he was totally innocent and so would the judge as soon as he had a chance to put on his case. The prosecution's case consisted of the testimony of the arresting officers who went to the defendant's residence in the Ninth Ward with a search warrant and took pictures of the backyard and cuttings from the plants growing in the backyard which the prosecution's botanist subsequently testified was cannabis satiba, and introduction of the deed of title to the property in defendant's name. At that point Judge Cocke strongly suggested the man seek counsel to help him, and pointed out to him that he did not have to take the stand. Notwithstanding such good counsel, the defendant told the judge that he had nothing to fear by taking the stand, and he did so. On the stand he explained that he raised canaries and other song birds at home for fun and profit, and that the cages had to be cleaned every day. He told the court that after his arrest, he did not understand how marijuana plants could be growing in his backyard, so he investigated and found that the product he had been feeding them contained marijuana seeds, which is why the birds were so happy and sang so much. He told the court that when he cleaned the cages, he took the pans out to the stoop leading to the backyard and simply pitched the droppings into the yard, and that must have been how this whole misunderstanding came about. As the prosecution rose to cross examine, Judge Cocke waved his hand in their direction, turned sweetly to the defendant, and told him he was greatly impressed with the defense he had mounted. In fact, he was so impressed that he was prepared to dismiss all charges against the defendant if he could answer just one question to the court's satisfaction. However, if he could not, not only would Judge Cocke find him guilty of all charges and impose the heaviest possible sentence, but he also would turn the case over to the prosecutor to bring a charge of perjury in connection with the trial. The defendant turned white, but at that point he could say nothing else but that he would be happy to answer the question. Judge Cocke picked up the State's exhibit, the pictures of the backyard, showed it to the defendant and asked him to explain that if his story was the absolute God's truth, how was it all those seeds thrown from the back porch landed in nice straight rows in the backyard as shown in the pictures? That's the origin of the phrase "a birdshit defense" – one which at first sounds pretty good until you prick the surface.

CHAPTER XI

SETTLEMENTS

Because most (the conventional wisdom is 90 to 95%) legal controversies are settled before trial, it is notable that there are few stories concerning settlement negotiations. One occurring about the time of World War I is a classic. It is the consummate offer made by William M. Peterman, an Alexandria attorney, to Gaston L. Porterie, at that time a Marksville attorney but later Louisiana attorney general and then a federal district judge. We are grateful to Judge John Duhé of New Iberia and Howard Gist of Alexandria for providing copies of the Peterman letter.

Peterman's letter, dated in 1917, presented this offer to Porterie:

> You have a claim of Camille Neck's for $100 value of a cow killed by train (I should have said alleged value) upon which you offer to take $75 in settlement. Mr. Quick, the Company's claim agent, is very much distressed by your figures. He wants to settle with your client without suit, if possible, but can never on earth obtain authority to pay $75. He strained himself to the point of exhaustion by offering $35, has lost his nerve, dropped out of the betting and wants me to jump in the imminent, deadly breach and offer you $50. This I now do, simply in the way of a compromise, the railroad company, in making this offer does not acknowledge liability. I say to you, confidentially of course, that the animal in question undoubtedly committed suicide. The statements furnished me show that she hid behind a cattle-guard fence, evidently by design and quietly awaited the approach of the train in order to leap in front of it and end her life. What her thoughts must have been as she thus calmly waited for death, we will not inquire. The subject is too painful. There must have been some powerful motive that actuated her in taking this dreadful course. Possibly she was afflicted with some incurable

disease and saw only a future of suffering. Possibly, again, she suffered from the pangs of unrequited love; or, it may be she sacrificed her virtue to the blandishments of some scoundrelly young bull of the neighborhood and could not survive the disgrace of exposure. Now, if you will take $50 I will see to it that this secret of her suicide will be sacredly guarded. If you decline it and the case is aired in the Courts, her family will be dishonored and her memory stained, and for this, your client will be answerable. But there is a practical side of this matter which may appeal to Mr. Neck if he is not susceptible to the appeals of sentiment. It is this: If you will take $50 he will get it now. If he sues and obtains a judgment, say for double the amount, when and how will he obtain payment. He cannot issue execution, for the railroad is in the hands of receivers. He must await action by a Federal Court. These courts move leisurely. You don't know the height and depth and the length and the breadth of the word "leisure," unless you have had dealings with a Federal Court. If your client insists on a $100 his grandchildren may enjoy disbursing it. If he takes $50 now, there is no telling how much it will yield if judiciously invested in cotton futures. Or, if he is not of a speculative turn, let him buy a heifer or two and he will have a herd of milk cows before any judgment he may secure will be collectible.

Think of these things, dear friend and let me hear from you.

Yours, very truly,

Wm. H. PETERMAN

"Valuing" and "devaluing" cattle is a technique not limited to defense attorneys. As one Mississippi defense attorney once remarked: "Nothing improves the pedigree of a Mississippi bull like a collision with an Illinois Central train."

Members of the Taylor, Porter firm in Baton Rouge submit this as a caveat to those inclined to send the "Dictated but not Read" letters we sometimes receive:

> Defense counsel, unimpressed by plaintiff's counsel's claim that in settling they should consider the possibility that the plaintiff also sustained a head injury, was a little perplexed to receive this letter from plaintiff's counsel:

> I am willing to settle the claim for $35,000. However, this offer is only open until August 1st. If I do not hear from you by that time, I will be forced to send my client to a New Roads surgeon to evaluate the additional claim for head injury.

René Curry of New Orleans contributes another interesting settlement offer letter; this one, for the claims of a couple who claimed to have lost their senses of taste and smell because a "defogger" was defective, encompassed 30 pages, and included this plea for damages for loss of sex between the couple:

> Perhaps the most "delicate" issue is the loss of sexual stimulation and awareness that any person loses because of an inability to smell and taste their partner. Of course, not even taking into account the body's own odors (phenomones), of what use is cologne and perfume as a sexual stimulant or inducer to one who cannot smell? Therefore, it does not seem unreasonable but to a couple who describe their sex life as an important and outstanding part of their lives, that an award of $500,000 each (to last a lifetime) would barely do any justice, i.e. assuming that sex is had for only a banker's year of 260 days and that the going rate of sex for hire is approximately $150, which means that at a minimum, sexual pleasure has a minimal gratification value of $150 per occurrence. Then over a year it would equal $39,000. The expected sexual life span of each in this day of enlightenment should be their life expectancy, or at least 90% of each's life expectancy, or 24.57 (90% or 27.3) years

for Mr. _____ and 35.01 (90% of 38.9) years for
Mrs. _____ . 24.5 X 39G's = $955,500 and 35.01 X
39G's = $1,365,390. A jury could easily round these
figures off to $500,000 each. Now this figure does not
accurately represent the loss of sexual pleasure as the
_____ are still capable of performing sexually,
but, it is just as their gourmet tastebuds no longer are able
to sustain any pleasure from eating a great meal, then so
too sex becomes merely "going through the motions."
Since humans have five senses then the loss of two of
these would be slightly over one-third. But, just as medical
science is still fully unaware of any sixth sense, medical
science also discounts the value of taste and smell say in
sexual endeavors. What I'm trying to say is that more
normally we associate the sense of sight and the tactile
senses with the pleasure derived from sex rather than the
lesser used senses such as taste and smell. Therefore,
perhaps we should discount the $500,00 by 2/5... which
will give us the benefit of the doubt and a figure of
$200,000 each.

The case did not settle and the jury "zeroed" the plaintiffs.

Some cases would be settled earlier if counsel made proper
allowance for the opposition's doubting. Consider this story from
Rene Curry of New Orleans.

I was defending a fairly typical accident which
occurred at an intersection on Airline Highway controlled
by traffic signal lights. Both the plaintiff ("Clarence") and
the tortfeasor were crossing Airline Highway in opposite
directions. When the light changed to green for both
drivers, the northbound tortfeasor and the southbound
plaintiff each proceeded forward. The tortfeasor, who had
activated his left turn signal early on, began making a left
turn across the path of the plaintiff in order to travel west
on Airline Highway, while the plaintiff moved slowly
forward intending to continue across Airline Highway.
The plaintiff allegedly had observed the tortfeasor's left

turn signal and slowed his vehicle almost to a stop, giving the tortfeasor the impression that he was going to permit the tortfeasor to complete his left turn. The tortfeasor assumed that that was what was intended and continued his turn. Plaintiff, believing that the tortfeasor was, in fact, not going to act on his invitation to complete his left turn, began to move ahead again, at approximately the same time as the tortfeasor began his turn. A collision resulted.

Since liability seemed to be clear, why was I even considering going to trial? First, because the plaintiff wanted my policy limits, payment of which I did not think was justified, and, second, I learned during the course of discovery that the plaintiff had been receiving Social Security disability benefits for a number of years based on "Statutory or Legal Blindness." He had extreme myopia and was color blind, and his vision, with best possible correction, was 20/200 in each eye. The Social Security Administration's records were replete with what I considered to be admissions against interest by the plaintiff, alluding to previous accidents and, more importantly, to the fact that he was considered by two of his former employers, his family and, to some extent, himself to be a danger to himself and to others when behind the wheel of a vehicle.

Shortly before trial, we settled the matter for a relatively minimal amount. When plainitiff's counsel, who throughout the pendency of the suit refused to subscribe to my theory that his client's "legal blindness" caused the accident, returned the executed Release and Motion of Dismissal, he added this handwritten post-script to his letter:

"P.S. Rene, you got me on this one. Clarence ran into my building when he came to get his check. He explained, 'Just didn't see the building.'"

Geoff Snodgrass of New Orleans submits this unusual story:

Three lawyers went to a local Orleans pub after work and spent considerable time there. One of them had brought his briefcase. When he excused himself briefly to answer the call of nature, the other two lawyers quickly filled his briefcase with bar peanuts. As luck would have it, he took the briefcase home and the next morning went to an 8 a.m. settlement hearing on a worker compensation claim. As he opened his briefcase, peanuts spilled onto the floor of the judge's chambers, prompting the judge to comment that he'd heard of settling cases for peanuts before, but that this was ridiculous.

Geoff identifies the "peanut offering" lawyer as Phelps Gay, past president of the Bar. Phelps was unavailable for comment.

CHAPTER XII

TITLE LAWYERING

Many lawyers, by accident or choice, spend much of their careers dealing with land titles. Here are some entertaining stores about that genre:

> In the lexicon of the Shreveport Bar's stories, one of the oldest is about a venerable and crusty practitioner whose title opinion work blossomed furiously during the Odessa oilfield boom in the northern part of Caddo Parish. Our practitioner, it is said, would order abstracts from the title company and, following their delivery to his office, would first stack the abstracts neatly on the floor. Next, he would then gingerly step, one foot at a time, from one side of the pile of abstracts to the other. Finally, he would turn to his secretary and start dictating his title opinion as follows:
>
> > Dear [client]: I have carefully gone over Abstract No. _____, and find good title vested in the name of...."
>
> Judge Jacques Weiner
Shreveport

Those lawyers who read abstracts often find interesting things. Some of the best are in Cajunland, where the oldtimers sometimes named their children after commercial products. Thus it was not uncommon to come across a Zenith Thibodeaux or a Hotpoint Broussard in the conveyance records. One name which baffled one examiner, however, was Regus Patoff Leblanc. The mystery was solved a few weeks later when the examiner, taking a break at a local restaurant, picked up a bottle of popular catsup and observed the manner in which the manufacturer had abbreviated on the label the words "Registered U.S. Patent Office."

Michael Bordelon of Mandeville recalls that as he worked his way through law school doing abstract work, one of the games he and his fellow co-workers played was locating and identifying odd or funny names from the East Baton Rouge property records. Once they found a Mr. "Phlegm,"and a "Robin Hood" who lived on Sherwood Forest Boulevard. The favorite, which Michael claims he has documented with a certified copy, contained an appearance clause in an act from the mid-60s: "Power P.C. Poon, married but once and then to Grace T. Poon, born Tang."

Anyone who examines titles for any significant period knows what is the worst job in the business – turning down a title previously approved by a fellow practitioner. Sometimes the alleged title defect is a serious one (one once impelled a law firm to execute a hold harmless agreement to another firm in exchange for not rejecting the title to a lot in a new subdivision), and sometimes it is deemed "nitpicking." On one such later occasion, a young lawyer in Baton Rouge called the elderly "dean" of the title bar and suggested that the "dean" had overlooked a flaw in approving a title. The "dean's" response: "Son, you can pick the strongest, healthiest man in Baton Rouge and if you look long enough, you'll find a pimple on his ass. I worry about boils, not pimples."

A lawyer who has approved a title does not take kindly to another lawyer's subsequent rejection of the title. Here's how Michael Bordelon learned that lesson:

> I was examining a title to property that had gone through a divorce and community property partition. However, the lawyer had included in the partition other property which was the separate property of the husband, acquired by inheritance prior to the marriage. In the judgment of court effecting the partition, the husband's separate property was included with the other community property. Although the separate property was adjudicated to the husband, I was concerned about the title, since co-ownership was the essence of a valid partition. Thus I required a quitclaim from the spouse. The drafting attorney ranted and raved, wondered aloud who was I to question his work, and emphasized the difficulty in obtaining the quitclaim. I insisted, however, and obtained the document.

Years later, I was returning from a Bar Convention in France and was sitting next to another Louisiana attorney. As lawyers do, we commenced to talking and complaining about the current state of the practice of law in Louisiana. He then related the story of some pedantic title examiner who called him, cited some "obscure provision in law" concerning a judgment of partition, and required him to go to great inconvenience to obtain a quitclaim. Since I was the pedant, I did not know how to respond. Finally, in a jocular tone, I said "Mr. Blank, I know exactly what you are talking about because I'm the attorney who called you on that title." From that point on, the flight home was very quiet.

A lawyer who was examining title to properties in a northern parish noticed that the tax sales were consistently held only 27, 28 or 29 days after publication of the required notice. The requirement was at least 30 days, thus the tax sales were null - if not absolutely, then relatively null. The lawyer subsequently met the Sheriff of the parish and pointed out to him this apparent nullity problem in his sales tax sales. The Sheriff chuckled and said: "I don't mind some bottom-feeder making a little interest on his money [if redeemed], but I'll be damned if one of my voters is going to lose his property at a tax sale." He had deliberately violated the statute so as to make the tax sales null to give his constituents the opportunity to let a smart lawyer show off his skills and save properties.

CHAPTER XIII

WEIRD CASES

Law students frequently complain that the hypothets by which they are tested are unrealistic and too outrageous to occur in real life. The fact is that most of those hypothets are taken from real life cases, and that, at least in the law, truth often is stranger than fiction. Every experienced lawyer has his or her memorable "weird case"; here are a couple we have gathered.

Smitty Landry of New Iberia provides us with this "True Hazard" story:

> The basis facts of this story can be verified. The lawsuit on which it is based can be found among the Civil Records of Acadia Parish. (All names of persons in this account are fictitious except the name "Hazard" and the name of Judge Nehrbass.)

> Suire was an elderly gentleman who lived in rural Acadia Parish with his wife, and he enjoyed visits from his friend, Hazard (his real given name). Hazard was an insurance salesman who came by regularly with his "debit book" to collect the small premiums paid by Suire on a funeral and burial insurance policy.

> On one of those visits Suire complained to Hazard that branches from a tree were brushing against the roof of Suire's house. He was afraid that the branches would damage the roof but did not know how to get the branches cut. Hazard told Suire that he had a power saw and offered to come by on Saturday morning to cut the branches.

> On the following Saturday Hazard came by, and with a ladder provided by Suire, climbed to the roof with his power saw in hand, started the saw and began to cut the branches. After a short while, Hazard realized that because of the steep pitch of the roof his footing was precarious and he was afraid to continue the cutting

without more support. He asked Suire if he had a rope, and Suire produced a long rope which Hazard took, tied one end of it around his waist, and threw the other end over the peak of the roof. Hazard could not see the other side of the roof so he asked Suire to pull the loose end, which had fallen to the ground on the other side of the roof, until the rope was taut and at that point to secure the end of the rope to a fixed object. Suire, without telling Hazard where he had secured it, tied the rope to the back bumper of Suire's pick-up truck, parked in the front driveway. Feeling the security of the rope around his waist, and believing it to be tied to a fixed object on the other side of the roof, Hazard resumed the job of cutting the branches of the tree with his chain saw.

A short time later Suire's wife came out of the house, her hair in curlers, and jumped into the pick-up truck for a trip to the grocery story. She started the truck and proceeded out of the driveway, unknowingly pulling the rope, with Hazard tied to the other end of it, jerking Hazard over the peak of the roof and onto the ground on the other side, and dragging him down the driveway until his screams caused her to stop. Remarkably, Hazard was not killed, but he received serious injuries, breaking bones in both legs and sustaining cuts, bruises and abrasions about his entire body. After a period of recuperation Hazard achieved a good recovery, without much permanent disability.

Nevertheless, Hazard expected to receive compensation for his damages, but he could not negotiate a settlement with Suire's insurers, the liability carrier of the truck and the liability carrier of Suire's home, as they were fighting about who had primary coverage. Thus it was necessary for Hazard to file suit, and he did so in Acadia Parish.

Even then, because of the warring insurance companies, a settlement could not be negotiated and the case was fixed for trial by jury. As the matter proceeded toward trial, a pre-trial conference was held in the chambers of Judge Douglas J. Nehrbass, well known for his light-hearted personality and sense of humor. The lawyers assembled for the conference, and, as is customary, the judge first wanted to hear what the case was all about. Hazard's lawyer began by relating to the judge in vivid detail the story of Hazard, Suire and Suire's wife. The lawyer began with the tale of the branch-cutting project and the use of the rope, portraying Hazard as a "Good Samaritan." He dramatically ended his story by painting an oral picture of the incident, with Mrs. Suire, her hair in curlers, getting into the pick-up truck and heading for the grocery store, pulling Hazard over the peak of the roof and dragging him screaming down the driveway behind her. He ended the tale with a recitation of the nature and extent of Hazard's injuries, including the usual lawyer hyperbole, and emphasizing Hazard's volunteer status and his complete freedom from fault.

On hearing the story, and forming their own mental images of the incident as it took place, the judge, his law clerk and the court reporter erupted into fits of uncontrollable laughter which they were unable to suppress for several minutes.

Finally, after the judge was able to compose himself, he interrupted the conference. He told the lawyers that they should settle the case because he had no doubt that the reaction of the jury to the story of Hazard, Suire and Mrs. Suire would be the same as that of the judge and his staff, and the members of the jury would be rolling in laughter on the floor of the jury box. The judge expressed the opinion that, with the courtroom levity which would undoubtedly be generated by the comedy of errors that took place, the lawyers would never get the full attention of the jury members or persuade them to give serious consideration to the important issues in the case.

Heeding the judge's advice, the lawyers promptly resolved their differences and the case was settled.

John Larry Lolley, long time city judge and now district judge in Monroe, contributes this story about how a routine misdemeanor battery case provided evidence of a modern American mystery:

It begins in the Swartz area of east Ouachita Parish. Swartz is the site of a number of newly developing subdivisions but is also the site of a number of "premium" trailer parks well known to the Ouachita Parish Sheriff's Department. A lovely couple resided in the Pleasant Dreams Mobile Home Park. They had been living together for seven years and had two children. (They had never exactly gotten around to getting married.) The poor lady suffered seizures from time to time and would have to be hospitalized in Monroe for treatment. A slight problem existed, however, in that the gentleman could not check her into the hospital because he was not related to her. They would always stop by her mother's trailer on the way to the hospital so she could go with her daughter and check her in.

One pleasant spring afternoon the lady began having a seizure and the gentleman knew it was time to go to the hospital. (He was home at the time because he was drawing worker's comp from his latest job.) They drove immediately to her mother's trailer. The gentleman entered the trailer, stopped first at the "fridge" to get a cold beer, and told Mother to "get her stuff" and come on. Mother was not exactly happy and advised him that she told them earlier that she would not leave to sign her daughter into the hospital until after 3:00 p.m. The reason for this was that the last of the classic "Soap Operas" she watched every day on television did not end until that time. Needless to say, this did not sit too well with the gentleman and he became a bit upset with Mother.

Mother testified that this had happened before, and she knew that he was going to attack her. She stated that as soon as she saw him start toward her, she jumped up from the lazy boy and picked up something with which to defend herself. She then stated she put it down and did not have time to get something else before he reached her and that he then "whipped up" on her.

To say the least I was a bit confused by this time. I asked her why she put down the object she had picked up to defend herself with when she knew what was about to happen. She calmly looked at me and stated: "I didn't have a choice, judge. I was not going to break my Elvis decanter over his worthless head." Absolute proof that the KING lives.

The final act to this little drama was that the mother asked me not to put the guy in jail because it would cause his worker's comp to be cut off.

Rene Curry of New Orleans submits this unusual story:

I tried a case in the Civil District Court many, many years ago involving a suit by the surviving wife of a middle aged man who died a natural death. The couple had operated a neighborhood bar in Algiers, Louisiana, for years, working together daily, living in an apartment above the bar, being together 24 hours a day. Needless to say, they were extremely close. Neither had any particular health problem and she could not accept the fact that her husband had died. She visited the neighborhood cemetery where he was interred on a daily basis and talked to her husband while standing in front of his raised tomb. There were several steps leading up to the marble slab that served as the closure for the front of the tomb.

It would be reasonable to assume that the husband never responded, that is, not until one day after several days of inclement weather, during which time the wife was unable to visit the cemetery. When she returned on the first clear day it was only to discover some reddish brown substance had worked its way onto the steps of the tomb from under the base of the marble facia. She later described seeing various types of horrible looking things in and around this gory-looking substance. On seeing this and believing that her husband was alive, she concluded that he cut himself while trying to escape from the tomb, whereupon she rubbed her hands, etc., into the substance, exclaiming that her husband was alive but lay injured within the tomb.

While all of this was going on, she heard what she believed to be her husband's voice, crying out, "Let me out of here, let me out of here," over and over again. As a result, she became a psychological wreck and sought psychiatric assistance.

Suit was filed against the funeral home for improper embalming procedures and the sale of a defective casket; against the manufacturer of the casket for the defective casket; against the manufacturer of the shell of the casket for a defective weld on a seam; and against the cemetery for failing to properly seal the tomb. Close examination disclosed that the reddish brown substance was a mixture of loose brick and mortar dust, to which the marble was attached, and had not emanated from within the casket. The case was tried to a 12-person jury, 10 of whom were women. Defense counsel feared that sympathy might prevail and result in an unjust verdict. The jury returned a verdict against the manufacturer of the shell of the casket for a pin-hole defect in the casket. All other defendants were exonerated.

Thus far, the story is not one likely to occasion any laughs. But there is more. The lady actually heard the voice which she mistakenly believed to be that of her husband. The sexton of the cemetery lived immediately across the street from the cemetery and in close proximity to the tomb in question. He had a caged mynah bird which would cry out often in clearly understood words: "Let me out of here, let me out of here!"

CHAPTER XIV

WHAT'S IT ALL ABOUT?

Those who deal with the law and the legal system are special people. Most special are the lawyers, who are, at worst, gunfighters, hired to pit their mouths and brains against the mouths and brains of the client's enemy and his or her lawyer. Sometimes the gunfight is in the courtroom and sometimes it is at the negotiation table, but make no mistake, it is a "fight."

Being gunfighters, lawyers generally develop certain qualities. One is a love of their chosen profession, and another is a healthy respect for their helpers and their opponents. To the authors, the following stories capture in part the uniqueness of the "gunfighter brethren." We begin with Vance Andrus' "Aphorisms," which say a lot to us and a lot about us.

APHORISM NO. I.   **DO RIGHT WOMAN, DO RIGHT MAN**

Attorneys are compulsive list makers. To navigate the complexities of day-to-day practice, they tend to make lists of other lawyers, and in doing so divide all lawyers into categories of two, such as smart/dumb, quick/slow, pleasant/nasty, etc. There is one list, however, which attorneys hold most dear. It is a list of "good guys" and "bad guys." Every day of our professional lives, every attorney we deal with immediately refers to this list and determines whether we should be held in esteem as a "good guy" or scorned as a "bad guy." In this business, as in almost no other, one's reputation precedes one. It is built on a daily basis of innumerable choices and decisions you make and put into play. If you treat other people with dignity, respect, honesty and forthrightfulness, you in return will be honored and respected by your peers. On the other hand, act toward your peers with deceit, dishonesty, anger, or vituperativeness, and you will be adjudged a "bad guy." The result of such a designation is both subtle and far reaching. It will permeate the court system, your opponents' actions towards you, and your ability to obtain and keep clients.

Your reputation is like a suit of armor: so light you cannot feel it unless you lose it; so strong that, asleep or awake, it will protect you from the lies and innuendos others may hurl at you for their own personal gain. Once you have built it, you should rely upon it and fear not what others may say about you, for you have earned your right to wear it.

APHORISM NO. II   **THE WORLD IS PERFECTLY ROUND**

Stated otherwise, "every dog has his day." In virtually every case there is an opportunity to slam your opponent, usually on some petty, minor matter which will affect your opponent personally but will not gain for you any great strategic leverage. Just know this: the world is perfectly round, and attorneys have very long memories. Do unto others as you would have them do unto you, for, in fact, they will.

APHORISM NO. III   **PICK YOUR BATTLES**

Many attorneys apparently believe that litigation should be a war of attrition, with one battle after another fought and the winner being determined by whoever is left standing at the end of the war. However, this is not an effective or efficient method of litigation, because few clients have the time, energy or money to pursue this strategy. Instead, you should fight very few battles, but be fully prepared to win every battle fought, particularly if it is fought before a judge. It is necessary to create the persona in the judicial system that you are an attorney who means business, that you do not waste court time or effort, and that when you show up for a hearing, you fully expect to win. Fight only those battles which will directly affect the outcome of the litigation, and only those you are convinced you can win. Otherwise, concede, conserve and give ground in order to fight later on an occasion of your own choosing.

APHORISM NO. IV   JUDGES ARE LAWYERS TOO

Review Aphorism number I. Judges makes lists just as attorneys do. They also are busy people who are easily distressed by unprepared, incompetent, or egotistical attorneys. Never go to court unprepared and always check your ego and your anger at the door before you enter the courtroom. Terrible things happen in courtrooms. Surprising, crushing, seemingly absurd rulings can, and often are, dropped on your head in trial and in motion practice. Generally, judges will tolerate incompetence, but they will never tolerate anger, excessive ego, or rudeness from a trial attorney. Your reputation precedes you, and judges talk to other judges.

APHORISM NO. V   CIVILIANS ARE NON-COMBATANTS

Someday, on the day before a big trial, your opponent will call and tell you that his 14 year child was just involved in an automobile accident, and he has to leave immediately for the hospital. He will ask you for a continuance and you had better give it to him. If you don't, he will get it from the judge anyway, and you will have violated one of the sacred principles of trial law:

never drag your opponent's family into the litigation. There are many reasons to fight a request for a continuance, but illness, death, or personal tragedy in your opponent's family are not among them.

APHORISM NO. VI   **YOUR MAMA DOESN'T LIVE HERE**

Your mama doesn't live here, clean up your own mess. If you miss an 8:00 a.m. Monday appointment because you forgot to check your calendar Friday afternoon, don't lie, or come up with some lame excuse about traffic on the expressway. And never, never, ever lie so as to blame your failings on your secretary. Lawyers and judges alike appreciate honesty. If you have made a mistake, admit it, apologize if appropriate, and move forward. No one said you had to be perfect.

APHORISM NO. VII   **THE OLE COON WALKS LAST IN THE WOODS AT NIGHT**

Ever so often the practice will afford you the opportunity to come into contact with one of the legends of the bar: an attorney whose success, reputation, power and influence tower over yours, as well as over most of the rest of the legal community. Relax. Enjoy their presence, for these attorneys are usually the most engaging, personable, and interesting persons you will ever meet. They tend to live life LARGE, work hard, play harder and enjoy life immensely. Watch them practice, take notes, and decide for yourself what it is about their personalities and attitudes that makes them special. Most of all, however, don't be intimidated. Instead, be prepared, be prompt, be courteous and be knowledgeable about your case, for there is precious little in this profession as rewarding as a good fight against a worthy opponent.

APHORISM NO. VIII   YOUR ONLY ALLY IS YOUR SECRETARY

If you want gratitude, buy a dog. If you want understanding, support, and appreciation for your efforts, turn not to your spouse. Unless he or she is also an attorney or a legal secretary, your spouse can never understand the pressures, difficulties and complexities of the day-to-day practice of law. Alternatively, if he or she is an attorney or legal secretary, then your spouse likely doesn't have time or energy to care about your problems. You only have one true ally, and that is your secretary.

Loyalty is a two way street. Do you expect your secretary there at 9:30 at night racing to finish a brief that you procrastinated dictating until the last day? If so, then when she comes to you the next week and says she has to take her son to the doctor, you better not quote to her the firm absentee policy. And never, never ever blame your secretary for your or even her own mistakes.

Finally, do not confuse fault with responsibility. You are ultimately responsible for the handling of your caseload, and, therefore, any discussion of whose "fault" it is that something wasn't done timely or properly is immaterial. Understand this: you cannot delegate responsibility, you can only delegate authority. Ultimate responsibility lies with you for the successful practice of law, and you cannot delegate it. What you can do, however, is delegate your authority to make decisions and take actions. If you have confidence in the competence of your associates, partners, secretaries or others, delegate to them as much authority as you deem appropriate to allow them to assist you in accomplishing your task. Having done so, however, take care not to criticize them every time they exercise that authority on your behalf.

What do we get out of it all? Judge John Duhé gives an insight with the following story:

Jimmy Helm called me into his office and told me to go to the courthouse and read the succession proceedings of all the deceased lawyers who had lived in that parish. When I asked what information he wanted me to get, he just said: "Go and read them and report back to me when you have." I did as he asked. Several days later, when I had completed the task, I returned with my notes to Jimmy. He asked: "What did you learn?" I looked through my notes and replied: "All of them apparently lived well, they had fine houses on the best streets in town. They were each active in their churches, and held offices in most of the civic clubs and fraternal organizations, and all served on bank boards and headed charitable organizations. But all except A and B died insolvent." "Exactly," he replied, "and A and B inherited money. Each lawyer was a respected member of the community who lived well, but none got rich. If you want to get rich, you are in the wrong profession. If you want to live well and be a respected member of the community and serve the citizens, you are in the right profession."

Gathering stories, we called upon Sam D'Amico, a great trial lawyer for over 60 years. He cautioned that most of his material lacks humor, for a good reason. Sam recalls: "After a juror, at the end of a trial 60 years ago, accused the lawyers, including me, of laughing in the courtroom, I have since not laughed in a courtroom in the presence of a jury."

Sam recalls that another time, during a lull in a jury trial, with the jury in the box, the judge told a joke. After the trial, two of the jurors who knew Sam came to him at the counsel table and wanted to know what to do with the judge. The moral: to the litigants and jurors, "it ain't funny."

One lawyer-to-lawyer missile which probably was not in jest was the following letter sent by one attorney to another. The names have been deleted:

> Mr. _____ :
>
> RE: School District Class Action?
>
> Dear Mr. _____ :
>
> I sincerely hope you don't think me forward for writing you informally like this. However, having limited experience in class action litigation, as well as many other areas of the law, I am always eager to learn from the masters. It was with that thought in mind that I read the transcript of the April 19, 1984 hearing before the Honorable _____ .
>
> In reading that transcript, I read your comments with particular interest. After reading your comments and considering them in the context of what transpired, I most certainly would love the pleasure of personally meeting you. You have got to be the greatest asshole that ever stepped into a court of law, and I would like to go to my blessed rewards knowing that I personally met the greatest at something.
>
> Respectfully yours,

What we do for a living has best been summarized by a famous trial lawyer, John W. Davis, with the following words:

"True, we build no bridges. We raise no towers. We construct no engines. There is little of all that we do which the eye of man can see. But we smooth over difficulties; we relieve stress; we correct mistakes; we take up other men's burdens and by our efforts we make possible the peaceful life of men in a peaceful state."

A recent order of a federal district judge sent in by Fritz Bott of New Orleans perhaps places all of this into focus. We reproduce it below in its entirety:

UNITED STATES DISTRICT COURT
FOR THE DISTRICT OF COLUMBIA

CITIZENS COAL COUNCIL, et al :

                       :

Plaintiffs,   :

                       :

      v.   : C i v i l
                          Action
                          No. 00-
                          274 (JR)

                       :

BRUCE BABBITT, Secretary, U.S. :
Department of the Interior,   :

                       :

Defendant,   :

                       :

      and   :

                       :

NATIONAL MINING ASSOCIATION :

:

Intervenor-Defendant   :

MEMORANDUM ORDER

The recent heated exchange between plaintiffs and intervenor on the subject of whether or not NMA should have filed a statement of material facts pursuant to Rule 56.1 or not, whether the Court has granted plaintiffs' motion for leave to file supplemental authority or not, whether the Court's own previous order is "authority" or not, etc., betrays a startling lack of sense of humor, or sense of proportion, or both, especially since it appears to be agreed that the facts relevant to this case are all in the administrative record. It is this 21st day of May, 2001.

ORDERED that NMA's Rule 56.1 statement is <u>not</u> "rejected," that it will remain of record, and that it may remain as "context" for MNA's arguments. And it is

FURTHER ORDERED that the parties lighten up.

The message from all of this is that good lawyers always take their work seriously but rarely take themselves and their confreres seriously. It's what one might expect of gunfighters.

INDEX OF CONTRIBUTORS

DO YOU HAVE A STORY that should have appeared in this collection? We'd like to include it in the second volume of *Louisiana Law: Legends and Laughs.*

Send your contributions to Prof. Frank L. Maraist, 330 Sunset Blvd., Baton Rouge, LA 70808, by mail or by fax (225) 819-8525 or by e-mail (cmaraist@aol.com).

NEED EXTRA COPIES OF *LEGENDS AND LAUGHS*?

Send $21.25 (*$14.95 plus $1.35 sales tax plus $4.95 shipping & handling*) per copy payable to:

> Birdfoot Delta Press
> 221 Florida Street
> Baton Rouge, LA 70801

Please allow 2-3 weeks for delivery.